STUMP

THE

GROWN-UP

APPLESAUCE PRESS

Kennebunkport, Maine

13-Digit ISBN: 9781604336566
10-Digit ISBN: 1604336560

This book may be ordered by mail from the publisher. Please include $5.99 for postage and handling. Please support your local bookseller first!

Books published by Cider Mill Press Book Publishers are available at special discounts for bulk purchases in the United States by corporations, institutions, and other organizations. For more information, please contact the publisher.

Applesauce Press is an imprint of
Cider Mill Press Book Publishers
"Where good books are ready for press"
PO Box 454
12 Spring Street
Kennebunkport, Maine 04046

Visit us on the Web! www.cidermillpress.com

Design by: Melissa Gerber
Typography: Archer, Festivo Letters, Hello Beautiful Marker, KG Second Chances, Microbrew two, Sedgwick Co, Thirsty Rough, and Minion Pro
Image Credits: Shutterstock.com

Printed in the United States
2 3 4 5 6 7 8 9 0
First Edition

TABLE of CONTENTS

Cool Science

Math Mania

Reading Room

Lunch & Recess

Around the World

After-School Activities

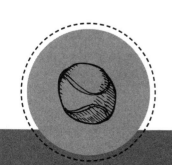

 # HOW to PLAY!

This book is divided into six "classes:" Cool Science, Math Mania, Reading Room, Lunch and Recess, Around the World, and After-School Activities. Each section ends with a lightning round of 25 true-or-false questions to really test your grown-ups! Don't forget to try for Extra Credit!

ONCE YOU'VE COMPLETED A TRUE-OR-FALSE LIGHTNING ROUND AT THE END OF EACH CLASS, USE THE FOLLOWING LEVELS TO SCORE:

0-5 **QUESTIONS RIGHT:** *Go Back to Second Grade!*

6-10 **QUESTIONS RIGHT:** *Nice Try... But Time to Repeat Grade Three!*

11-20 **QUESTIONS RIGHT:** *Lucky for you, Fourth Grade Wasn't So Bad— Back You Go!*

21+ **QUESTIONS RIGHT:** *Congratulations! You Might Be Ready for Middle School!*

But don't worry if you'd prefer to skip around or not keep score. How you play is up to you and your family!

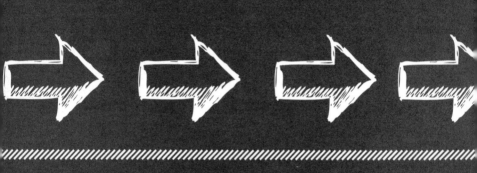

Cool SCIENCE

THE DINOSAUR KINGDOM

1. Which of the following dinosaurs is the tallest:

a. The Giraffatitan

b. The Tyrannosaurus rex

c. The Allosaurus

d. The Camarasaurus

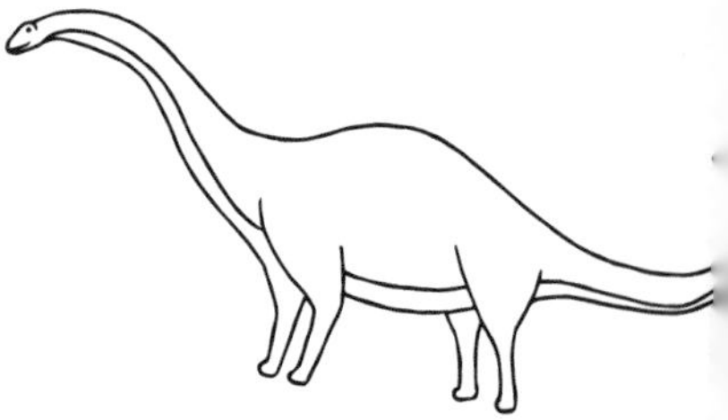

2. How long are the arms of the T. rex compared to its massive height of 20 feet?

3. How many teeth does the Velociraptor have?

a. 55

b. 40

c. 80

d. 75

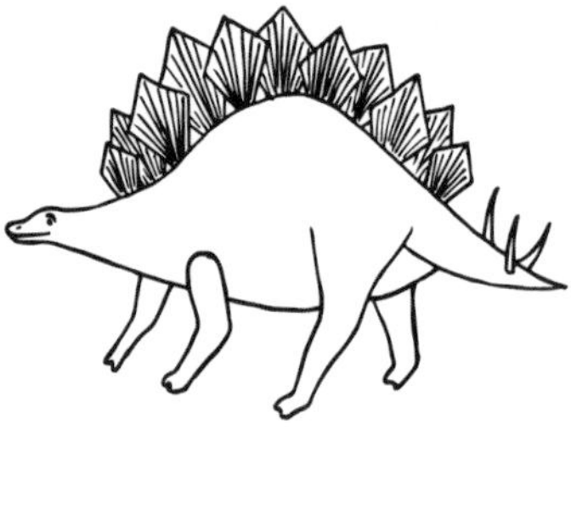

ANSWER KEY 1. a—The Giraffatitan was believed to be approximately 50 feet tall. 2. 3 feet 3. c

4. Which dinosaur is the smallest:

   a. The Troodon

   b. The Heterodontosaurus

   c. The Coelurus

   d. The Oviraptor

5. What is the believed function of the large curved crest on the head of the Parasaurolophus?

6. What does "saurus" mean in English?

7. What does "phale" mean in English?

8. Which time period came first, the Triassic or the Jurassic?

9. Which time period came first, the Cretaceous or the Jurassic?

ANSWER KEY 4. b **5.** To communicate over vast distances with sounds similar to those of a whale. **6.** "Lizard." **7.** "Head." **8.** The Triassic—251 to 199 million years ago. **9.** The Jurassic—199 to 145 million years ago.

11

10. How fast can the Tyrannosaurus run?

    a. 50 mph

    b. 25 mph

    c. 30 mph

    d. 45 mph

11. What distinguishing feature does the Stenopelix have?

12. The Heterodontosaurus has how many different kinds of teeth?

13. The Euoplocephalus has what distinguishing feature?

14. Which of the following was discovered first:

    a. The Archaeopteryx

    b. The Rhoetosaurus

    c. The Tyrannosaurus rex

    d. The Centrosaurus

15. The Prenocephale is known for its thick what?

16. How many pounds of flesh could a Tyrannosaurus rex can bite through?

17. Did the Coelophysis snack on its own kind?

PLANET EARTH

1. How much of an iceberg is typically above water level?

   a. One-quarter

   b. One-half

   c. One-sixth

   d. One-ninth

2. About how deep is the Earth's crust?

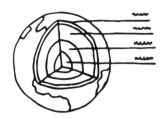

    a. 2 miles

    b. 4 miles

    c. 10 miles

    d. 25 miles

3. What it the equatorial circumference of the Earth?

    a. About 24,000 miles

    b. About 32,000 miles

    c. About 40,000 miles

    d. About 48,000 miles

4. About what percent of the land mass of Earth is covered in ice?

    a. 5%

    b. 10%

    c. 15%

    d. 18%

5. What percentage of the Earth is covered by water?

  a. 48%

  b. 63%

  c. 71%

  d. 82%

6. What are the five states that border the Gulf of Mexico?

7. Is the deepest part of the Atlantic Ocean more or less than 35,000 feet?

8. How many square miles is the Indian Ocean?

  a. 15 million

  b. 20 million

  c. 29 million

  d. 43 million

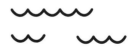

9. What is the average salt content of the oceans?

    a. 1%

    b. 3.5%

    c. 4.8%

    d. 6%

10. In what state is the source of the Mississippi River?

11. In the open sea, about how far can sunlight reach underwater?

    a. 1,280 feet

    b. 2,480 feet

    c. 3,280 feet

    d. 4,680 feet

12. Which high cloud type indicates that it's raining?

    a. Cirrus

    b. Cirrocumulus

    c. Cirrostratus

    d. None of the above

13. What hurricane devastated New Orleans in 2005?

    a. Hugo

    b. Katrina

    c. Rita

    d. Wilma

14. In what month is Arbor Day?

15. What do coniferous trees produce instead of flowers?

OUTER SPACE AND BEYOND!

1. Which celestial body was considered a planet until 2006, when it was reclassified as a dwarf planet?

2. What do we call a star that is formed when a supernova explodes?

3. What are the four stages of the moon?

4. The Apollo space program successfully placed what man on the moon in 1969?

5. The core, radiative zone, convective zone, and photosphere are all parts of what celestial body?

6. What is a meteoroid called when it enters Earth's atmosphere?

7. Newton's first law of motion says that an object at rest tends to do what?

8. Newton's third law of motion says that for every action there is an equal and opposite what?

9. What is defined as "force applied over distance"?

10. What equals mass times acceleration?

AMPHIBIANS, REPTILES, SEA CREATURES, AND MAMMALS

1. Match the animal to the name of its habitat:

1) Penguin   a. Lodge
2) Beaver   b. Nest
3) Wolf   c. Lair
4) Ostrich   d. Rookery

2. Match the animal to its young:

1) Elephant   a. Kid

2) Fox   b. Foal

3) Horse   c. Cub

4) Goat   d. Calf

3. Are mammals warm-blooded or cold-blooded?

4. Which tends to be smaller, a black bear or a polar bear?

5. Which tends to have a shorter coat, a black bear or a grizzly bear?

6. How many toes does a black bear have on each paw?

7. Is a polar bear's skin white?

ANSWER KEY 2. 1. d; 2. c; 3. b; 4. a **3.** Warm-blooded **4.** Black bear **5.** Black bear **6.** Five **7.** No—it's black.

8. Koalas and wallabies are *diprotodonts*, which means:

  a. Their feet and hands are different shapes

  b. They have shorter front limbs than back limbs

  c. They are marsupials with two incisor teeth in their lower jaw

  d. They eat eucalyptus

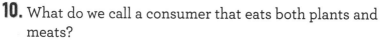

9. The lion is the second largest cat. What's the first?

10. What do we call a consumer that eats both plants and meats?

11. Which is larger, a gray wolf or a red wolf?

12. Does a woodchuck chuck wood?

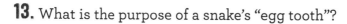

13. What is the purpose of a snake's "egg tooth"?

ANSWER KEY 8. c 9. Tiger 10. an omnivore 11. Gray 12. No 13. To help a newborn snake break through its egg in order to hatch.

21

14. What is the longest snake in the world?

   a. The Burmese Python

   b. The California Kingsnake

   c. The Common Boa

   d. The Reticulated Python

15. A group of dolphins is called a what?

16. Which is larger, the great white shark or the whale shark?

17. What are baby sharks known as?

18. What is a favorite food among great hammerhead sharks?

19. How long is the average great white shark?

20. What differentiates porpoises from dolphins?

21. What beautiful creature makes an appearance as easy-going dad, Crush, in *Finding Nemo*?

22. Do killer whales prefer living in solitude or with a family?

23. What is the biggest predator of the lion's mane jellyfish?

24. What gentle giant is often called the "sea cow"?

25. Which is characteristically more aggressive, the tiger shark or the sand tiger shark?

ANSWER KEY 20. Porpoises have shorter snouts and are smaller and rounder than dolphins. 21. The hawksbill sea turtle 22. With a family—usually up to 40 total killer whales. 23. The sea anemone 24. The manatee 25. The tiger shark

26. Where are the nostrils of a hammerhead shark located?

27. Which is the deadliest:

a. The sea wasp

b. The great white shark

c. The barrel jellyfish

d. The manta ray

28. How many eyes does the sea wasp have?

29. What makes the swell shark similar to a dog?

30. What shark is called "the garbage can of the sea"?

ANSWER KEY 26. At the tips of the extensions on either side of its head. 27. a—the venom from one sea wasp is enough to kill up to 60 adult humans. 28. 24 total—four sets of eye-clusters. 29. It barks like one when threatened. 30. The tiger shark, as it is known to eat almost anything—even inanimate objects.

31. What can the shade of a tiger shark's stripes tell you?

32. Which is the largest land-dwelling salamander?

a. The Barred Tiger Salamander

b. The Italian Fire Salamander

c. The Spotted Salamander

d. The California Slender Salamander

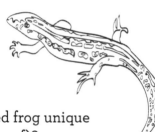

33. What makes the bell's argentine horned frog unique (and a frog that humans should be wary of)?

34. What is the defense of many lizards against predators?

35. What is unique about the bathroom habits of the Chinese soft-shelled turtle?

ANSWER KEY 31. How old it is: the darker the stripes, the younger the shark is: the lighter the stripes, the older the shark is. 32. a 33. Its huge mouth with tooth-like projections. 34. They can detach their tail, distracting a predator while they escape. 35. It urinates through its mouth (yuck!)

25

36. What makes a frog different from a toad (apart from physical characteristics)?

37. What do bright colors in reptiles usually indicate?

38. Which frog is the most poisonous:

   a. The Golden Mantella
   b. The Cuban Tree Frog
   c. The Golden Poison Dart Frog
   d. The Red-Eyed Tree Frog

39. How do bearded dragons usually communicate?

40. What is the average length of the komodo dragon?

   a. 10 feet
   b. 7 feet
   c. 15 feet
   d. 5 feet

41. What do leopard geckos do with the layers of skin that they shed?

42. What turtle has a two-part name (the same word twice) and looks more like browning leaves than a turtle?

43. What large toad is known for the flame pattern on its stomach?

44. What species was the main character of the Paramount Pictures movie *Rango*?

45. What do bed bugs eat?

46. Where do carpenter ants like to make their homes?

ANSWER KEY 41. Eat them. 42. The mata mata 43. The oriental fire-bellied toad 44. The panther chameleon 45. Blood 46. Damp wood

27

47. What is the lifespan of the rose tarantula?

    a. 10 years

    b. 5 years

    c. 30 years

    d. 20 years

48. What part of the world does the emperor scorpion dwell in?

    a. Egypt

    b. India

    c. West Africa

    d. Australia

49. How many pairs of eyes does the jumping spider have?

50. Where do monarch butterflies migrate to in the winter?

    a. Mexico

    b. The Mediterranean islands

    c. The Philippines

    d. West Africa

EXTRA CREDIT!

1. The mass of Jupiter is how many times larger than the mass of the Earth?

   a. 1250 times

   b. 318 times

   c. 500 times

   d. 750 times

2. When was Pluto discovered?

   a. 1755

   b. 1849

   c. 1899

   d. 1930

3. When William Herschel discovered Uranus in 1781, what did he think it was?

4. Ceres was the name of the first discovered what?

5. About how hot is the surface of the sun?

   a. 10,000 degrees F

   b. 50,000 degrees F

   c. 100,000 degrees F

   d. 1,000,000 degrees F

6. Which is hotter, the surface or the center of the sun?

7. What element makes up about 75% of the sun?

8. What is the second most common element in the sun?

   a. Helium

   b. Oxygen

   c. Hydrogen

   d. Calcium

9. Is it a solar or lunar eclipse when moon is positioned between the sun and the Earth?

10. When is the next total solar eclipse to be visible from the continental United States expected?

a. December 9, 2020

b. March 4, 2017

c. August 12, 2017

d. January 18, 2019

11. Is Mercury's year shorter or longer than Earth's?

12. Is there ever a second full moon in a month?

13. On what planet is the largest volcano in our solar system?

a. Mars

b. Mercury

c. Jupiter

d. Pluto

14. Which gets closer to the Earth, Venus or Mars?

15. About how old is Earth's moon?

    a. 8.8 million years

    b. 4.6 billion years

    c. 19.2 billion years

    d. 120.7 billion years

16. Is Pluto—which used to be considered a planet—smaller or larger than Earth's moon?

17. On what planet did the *Pathfinder* probe land in 1997?

18. How many crew members died when the shuttle Columbia exploded?

19. How many moons does Mars have?

ANSWER KEY 14. Venus 15. b 16. smaller 17. Mars 18. Seven 19. two—Phobos and Deimos

20. Jupiter's Great Red Spot was first seen in what year by astronomer Giovanni Cassini?

    a. 1665

    b. 1765

    c. 1865

    d. 1895

21. What is the second largest planet in our solar system?

22. How many Earth years long is a Jupiter year?

    a. 3x

    b. 5x

    c. 9x

    d. 12x

23. Only one U.S. President has attended a space shuttle launch. Name him.

24. Astronaut Wally A. Schirra has the distinction of being the only astronaut to fly in what three missions?

25. How old is the sun's light by the time it reaches Earth?

26. How many flights did the shuttle *Columbia* make?

    a. 38

    b. 28

    c. 18

    d. 8

27. How many flights did *Endeavour* make?

    a. 9

    b. 19

    c. 29

    d. 39

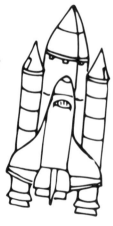

ANSWER KEY 24. Mercury, Gemini and Apollo 25. about eight minutes 26. b 27. b

28. Cassini is the largest interplanetary spacecraft ever built. What planet is it headed for?

29. Soviet cosmonaut Gherman Titoy was the youngest person to travel to outer space. How old was he when he took the flight in 1961?

a. 15

b. 20

c. 25

d. 30

30. The following five countries were the first to launch satellites. Put them in order beginning with the first to launch: France, USA, China, USSR, Japan

31. What space word is short for quasi-stellar object?

32. What is a star called that has exhausted its core hydrogen and is now fusing hydrogen outside the core?

33. Subtract the number of stars in the Little Dipper from the number of stars in the Big Dipper. What is the result?

34. 3.261 light years equals what?

35. The first spaceship rendezvous was in 1965 between Gemini 6 and Gemini 7. How close did the two ships come to each other?

    a. 6 inches

    b. 6 feet

    c. 6 yards

    d. 6 miles

36. On Earth's moon, Mare Tranquillitatis is also known as what?

37. What were the first living creatures sent into space from Earth?

38. How did the first monkey in space, Albert II, die?

a. He ran out of oxygen.

b. His parachute didn't work properly.

c. He had a heart attack.

d. Old age.

39. How did the first mouse in space die?

a. Its rocket disintegrated.

b. It was hit by a piece of equipment.

c. Electrical shock.

d. Old age.

40. Is Appleton's layer the highest or lowest region of the Ionosphere?

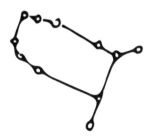

41. What golf club head did Alan Shepard use when he hit a ball on the Moon in 1971?

a. driver

b. 3-iron

c. 6-iron

d. pitching wedge

42. How many men have walked on the surface of the Moon?

a. 6

b. 8

c. 10

d. 12

43. Which star is closest to our sun?

a. Proxima Centauri

b. Alpha Centauri

c. Bernard's Star

d. None of the above

44. How old was John Glenn when, in 1998, he became the oldest person in space?

    a. 62

    b. 68

    c. 72

    d. 77

45. Which of these famous people has an asteroid named after them?

    a. Alfred Hitchcock

    b. Mister Rogers

    c. Lance Armstrong

    d. all of the above

46. What are the most common colors in an aurora?

    a. blue and gold

    b. brown and yellow

    c. red and pink

    d. pink and green

47. Haley's Comet is expected to be visible from Earth in...

    a. 2061

    b. 2030

    c. 2019

    d. Never again

48. What did an astrolabe do?

    a. calculate tides

    b. calculate the positions of stars

    c. find due north

    d. none of the above

49. When did Edwin Powell Hubble discover the distance between galaxies?

    a. 1900s

    b. 1910s

    c. 1920s

    d. 1930s

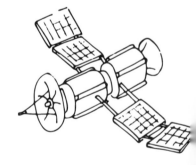

50. According to the big bang theory, about how many years ago did the big bang occur?

a. 56 million

b. 1.9 billion

c. 5.6 billion

d. 13.7 billion

51. About how many suns in the Milky Way?

a. 50-100

b. 1,000-10,000

c. 10,000-100,000

d. 100-400 billion

52. The larger a star's mass, the longer or shorter its lifespan?

53. A star collapses and becomes a white dwarf when all of its core hydrogen is converted into...

a. silicone

b. oxygen

c. helium

d. proteins

54. How many asteroids did NASA's *Galileo* pass on its way to Jupiter?

a. two

b. 20

c. 200

d. 2000

55. During long periods in space, does an astronaut's muscle mass decline or increase?

56. During long periods in space, does an astronaut's muscle blood volume increase or decrease?

57. How many images has the Wise spacecraft taken?

    a. 6 million

    b. 2 million.

    c. 650

    d. 1250

58. When were the first planets orbiting other stars (besides the Sun) discovered?

    a. 1845

    b. 1912

    c. 1956

    d. 1992

59. What belt are Pluto and its moons in?

    a. The Transis belt

    b. The Kuiper belt

    c. The Agriss belt

    d. The Orion belt

60. The letters after the name of an extrasolar planet indicates what?

a. its distance from Earth

b. the year it was discovered

c. the order it was discovered

d. none of the above.

61. Are most of the discovered exoplanets—planets outside our solar system—smaller or larger than the Earth?

62. Which of the following is not a moon of Pluto?

a. Charon

b. Hydra

c. Nix

d. Nox

63. Whose rockets were the first to reach the border of space?

a. Russia

b. Germany

c. U.S.

d. China

64. What was the name of the Canadian Space Agency robot taken to the International Space Station by *Endeavour* in 2008?

a. Dieter

b. Dextre

c. Diodier

d. Doctre

65. About how fast does a satellite in low orbit travel?

a. five miles per hour

b. five miles per minute

c. five miles per second

d. 50 miles per second

66. What was the first space shuttle to fly as part of the Space Transportation System (STS-1)

67. How long after the *Challenger* explosion did NASA keep astronauts out of space?

a. one year

b. three years

c. five years

d. seven years

68. Who was first in space, first African-American Guion S. Bluford or first woman Sally Ride?

69. Which launched first, the *Discovery* or the *Atlantis*?

70. Where was the *Magellan* probe aimed?

a. Mars

b. Venus

c. Mercury

d. Saturn

71. The first three-person spacewalk was part of what shuttle's mission?

a. *Endeavour*

b. *Discovery*

c. *Enterprise*

d. *Columbia*

72. In what year did the shuttle *Atlantis* first dock with the Russian Mir station?

a. 1993

b. 1995

c. 1998

d. 2001

73. Which astronaut revisited space as part of the 1998 *Discovery* mission?

a. Neil Armstrong

b. John Glenn

c. Yuri Gagarin

d. David Wolfe

74. Which shuttle made the first human flight to the International Space Station?

a. *Endeavour*

b. *Discovery*

c. *Enterprise*

d. *Columbia*

TURN THE PAGE FOR A TRUE-OR-FALSE LIGHTNING ROUND!

HERE'S HOW TO GRADE A GROWN-UP:

0-5 QUESTIONS RIGHT: *Go Back to Second Grade!*

6-10 QUESTIONS RIGHT: *Nice Try... But Time to Repeat Grade Three!*

11-20 QUESTIONS RIGHT: *Lucky for you, Fourth Grade Wasn't So Bad—Back You Go!*

21+ QUESTIONS RIGHT: *Congratulations! You Might Be Ready for Middle School!*

1. True or false: No one has ever been struck by lightning more than five times.

2. True or false: More than half of the Nile is in Egypt.

3. True or false: Some snakes are live-bearing, meaning their young do not hatch from eggs.

4. True or false: Elephants can run faster than 25 mph.

5. True or false: A red kangaroo can reach 40 mph.

6. True or false: All zebras have the same stripe pattern.

7. True or false: A skunk's skin is striped.

8. True or false: The blood python is named as such because it drinks the blood of mammals.

9. True or false: The barracuda can swim up to 35 miles per hour.

10. True or false: The giant guitarfish is harmless to humans.

11. True or false: A great white shark can live for over 70 years.

12. True or false: Despite the name, killer whales belong to the dolphin family.

13. True or false: The manta ray can grow to up to 23 feet wide.

ANSWER KEY 8. False—its name comes from its red coloring. 9. False—but 27 miles per hour is still impressive! 10. True 11. True 12. True 13. True

51

14. True or false: The male walrus can weigh up to 4,000 lbs.

15. True or false: The bull shark is known to be more aggressive toward humans than the great white.

16. True or false: The saliva of a komodo dragon is poisonous.

17. True or false: There are more than 10,000 species of mammals in the world.

18. True or false: the panther chameleon's eyes can move independently of each other.

19. True or false: Daffodils grow to face the sun.

20. True or false: The *Archaeopteryx* is believed to be an ancestor of modern bird species.

21. True of false: Despite playing a big role in the film *Jurassic Park*, the Tyrannosaurus rex actually lived in the Cretaceous Period.

22. True or false: The *Andesaurus* is one of the smallest dinosaurs ever discovered.

23. True or false: All centipedes have approximately 100 legs.

24. True or false: Earwigs make their home in the ears of mammals.

25. True or false: The snail is not actually an insect.

ANSWER KEY 21. True 22. False—it is actually one of the largest. 23. False—the number of legs ranges from 15 pairs to 191 pairs. 24. False—despite the name, earwigs do not live in ears. 25. True

53

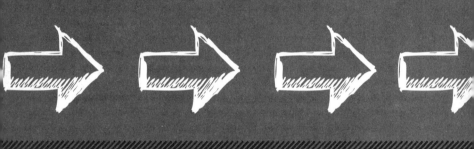

Math MANIA

ARITHMETIC WHIZ

1. How many centimeters are in one inch?

2. 36 inches equals how many feet?

3. What is the name for 10100 ?

4. How many quarts are there in a gallon?

5. What is slightly longer: 365 days, or the time it takes the earth to orbit the sun?

6. How many meters are in 1 kilometer?

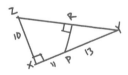

7. Whose theorum says that if you square the lengths of the two short sides of a triangle and add them together, the result is the square of the length of the longest side—the hypotenuse?

8. Angles less than 90 degrees are acute, and angles between 90 and 180 degrees are called what?

9. What law or property is represented by a(b+c) = ab+ac?

10. A hollow cube is made up of how many squares?

11. What is the formula to find the area of a rectangle?

12. What is the formula to find the circumference of a circle?

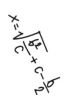

13. What do we call a number that reads the same backwards and forwards?

ANSWER KEY 7. Answer : Pythagoras' theorum 8. obtuse 9. distributive property 10. six 11. length times width 12. 2 times pi (3.14) times the radius 13. palindrome

57

14. Who was the first scientist to realize that the laws of the universe are mathematical and argued that the planets go around the sun?

15. What do we call a sequence of numbers in which each following number is the sum of the previous two?

16. Who was the first mathematician to use letters to represent unknown quantities in equations?

17. Who is known for coming up with the famous equation E = mc2?

18. What is the word for the science of codes and code breaking?

19. 40 feet = ___ yards

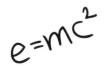

20. 8 pounds = ___ ounces

21. 23 centimeters and 3 millimeters = ___ millimeters

22. 3,000 centimeters = ___ meters

23. Find the area and perimeter of a rectangle that is 9 inches long and 5 inches wide.

24. Find the area and perimeter of a rectangle that is 11 yards long and 7 yards wide.

25. Find the area of a triangle with sides of 7 inches and a height of 5.4 inches.

26. Find the volume of a rectangular prism with sides of 2, 4, and 4 inches.

ANSWER KEY 20. 128 21. 233 22. 30 23. Area is 45 inches; perimeter is 28 inches 24. Area is 77 yards; perimeter is 36 yards 25. Area is 18.9 inches 26. Volume is 32 inches

59

ORDER OF OPERATIONS

1. What does PEMDAS stand for?

2. 6 x 10 =

3. 7 x 10 =

4. 8 x 10 =

5. 9 x 10 =

6. 10 x 10 =

7. 12 x 66 =

4×1 = 4
4×2 = 8
4×3 = 12
4×4 = 16
4×5 = 20
4×6 =

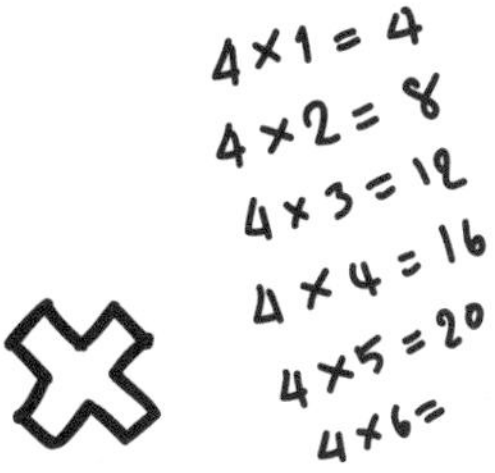

8. 13 x 98 =

9. 10 x 1.5 =

10. 1.3 x 1.8 =

11. 3.4 x 4 =

12. 5.5 x 5 =

13. 16÷ 8 =

14. 33÷ 11 =

15. ___÷ 5 = 1

ANSWER KEY } 8. 1,274 9. 15 10. 2.34 11. 13.6 12. 27.5 13. 2 14. 3 15. 5

16. 49 ÷ ___ = 7

17. 420 ÷ 10 =

18. 64 ÷ 2 =

19. 2710 ÷ 5 =

20. 67 ÷ 13 =

21. 548 ÷ 7 =

22. 2,389 ÷ 300 =

23. (763 − 4) x 6 + 8 =

24. (13 + 34) - 4 x 6 + 22 =

25. 3 x (1/4 + 2/4) – 610 =

26. (4 x 2) – (5/9 + 8/9) =

FRACTION AND FACTORING FUN

1. ½ = 10/___

2. 80/90 is greater or less than ¾?

3. 45/55 is greater or less than ¾?

4. 2/4 + ¾ =

5. 15 - 4/5 =

6. 3 + 6/15 =

7. What is 0.45 as a fraction?

8. What is 1.75 as a fraction?

9. What is 13/100 in decimals?

10. What is 13/14 in decimals?

11. List the prime factors of 76

12. List the prime factors of 45

13. List the prime factors of 39

14. List the prime factors of 90

WORD PROBLEMS

1. Lexi had 578 Legos but then her dog ate 147 of them. How many Legos does she have now?

2. TJ had $1 million, but then he spent $999, and then spent $32,222 more. How much money does TJ have left?

3. Mary, her brother, her mother, and her father each have one 6-ounce glass of orange juice each morning. If her mother buys one gallon of orange juice, how many whole servings of orange juice will they get out of the gallon? How many mornings will one gallon of orange juice last them?

4. Ryan's mother was born in 1967. In what year did she celebrate her 25th birthday?

EXTRA CREDIT!

1. What name is given to a triangle with two equal sides?

2. What name is given to a triangle with three equal sides?

3. What name is given to a triangle with no equal sides?

4. Pi is the ratio of what two measurements?

5. Isaac Newton, in addition to discovering gravity, invented what branch of mathematics?

    a. Algebra

    b. Calculus

    c. Geometry

    d. Trigonometry

ANSWER KEY 1. isosceles 2. equilateral 3. scalene 4. circumference and diameter of a circle 5. b

6. In geometry, what three letters are used at the end of a proof to mean, "It has thus been proven"?

a. ABC

b. GRE

c. PDQ

d. QED

7. Match the shape to the number of sides.

1. Ellipse   a. 0

2. Nonagon   b. 4

3. Pentagon   c. 5

4. Rhombus   d. 9

8. How many degrees are in a right angle?

9. How many degrees are in a circle?

10. What well-known company got its name from the word for 1 followed by 100 zeroes?

11. A line, in geometry, has no fixed beginning or ending point. What has a fixed starting point but no ending point?

12. What musical name is given to a line which passes through two points on a circle without passing through the center?

13. Match the Roman numeral to its value.

1. C   a. 1
2. D   b. 5
3. I   c. 10
4. L   d. 50
5. M   e. 100
6. V   f. 500
7. X   g. 1000

14. A diagram using overlapping circles to illustrate common members of different sets is named for what mathematician?

a. Euler

b. Leibniz

c. Newton

d. Venn

15. Your flight is supposed to leave the airport at 2:03 p.m., but you need to be at the airport at least 2 ½ hours early. What is the latest time that you may arrive?

16. What children's author described the basic arithmetic operations as "Ambition, Distraction, Uglification and Derision"?

   a. Lewis Carroll

   b. A.A. Milne

   c. Shel Silverstein

   d. E.B. White

17. What satirist defined "New Math" as "so very simple that only a child can do it"?

   a. Tom Lehrer

   b. Seth McFarlane

   c. Anna Russell

   d. Mort Sahl

18. What set of numbers is defined as those numbers which can be written as fractions?

a. decimal

b. natural

c. rational

d. real

19. A number whose factors other than itself add up to the original number is called what?

a. cardinal

b. imaginary

c. irrational

d. perfect

20. Which U.S. president independently proved the theorem governing the lengths of the sides of a right triangle?

a. Thomas Jefferson

b. Franklin Pierce

c. James Garfield

d. Woodrow Wilson

$$A = (a+c).h / 2$$

21. What is the longest side of a right triangle called?

22. What term is given to two angles that combine to form a right angle?

23. What term is given to two angles that combine to form a straight line?

24. What term is given to an angle of more than 180 degrees?

25. What term is given to a line that is steadily approached, but never reached, by a curve?

a. asymptote

b. axis

c. hyperbola

d. parabola

26. What Greek letter signifies the addition of numbers in a defined series?

a. Beta

b. Eta

c. Sigma

d. Theta

27. How many sides in a rhombus?

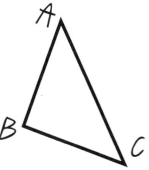

28. What former sitcom star earned her degree in mathematics, and has written three bestsellers urging middle-school girls to have confidence in their math skills?

a. Melissa Joan Hart

b. Danica McKellar

c. Susan Olsen

d. Tina Yothers

29. What talking toy sparked a controversy when it was programmed to say, "Math class is tough"?

a. Baby Alive

b. Barbie

c. Talking Tina

d. Teddy Ruxpin

$$(a + b + c)2 = a2 + b$$

30. A technique for double-checking arithmetic is called "casting out" what number?

a. sevens

b. eights

c. nines

d. tens

31. Computer science often uses base-16 numbers, also called what?

a. binary

b. decimal

c. hexadecimal

d. quattuordecimal

$$c2 + 2(ab + ac + bc)$$

$$Na-O-N\overset{O}{\underset{O}{}}\qquad CH_3-C\overset{O}{\underset{OH}{}}$$

$$c^2 = a^2 + b^2$$

$$y' = y$$

$$\int_0^1 x^5\,dx = \lim_{n\to\infty} \sum_{i=0}^{n-2}\left(\frac{i}{n}\right)^2 \cdot \frac{1}{n}$$

$$(a+b)^2 = a^2 + 2ab + b^2$$

$$2 \times 2 = 5 \qquad 2 \times 2 = 4$$

$$\triangle ABC \sim \triangle EFC \qquad x^3 + y^3 < z$$

TURN THE PAGE FOR A TRUE-OR-FALSE LIGHTNING ROUND!

HERE'S HOW TO GRADE A GROWN-UP:

0-5 QUESTIONS RIGHT: *Go Back to Second Grade!*

6-10 QUESTIONS RIGHT: *Nice Try... But Time to Repeat Grade Three!*

11-20 QUESTIONS RIGHT: *Lucky for you, Fourth Grade Wasn't So Bad— Back You Go!*

21+ QUESTIONS RIGHT: *Congratulations! You Might Be Ready for Middle School!*

MATH MANIA: LIGHTNING ROUND!

1. 1 mile measures 5,280 feet.

2. A type of triangle in which two sides and two angles are equal is called a scalene triangle.

3. The distance around the edge of a square or a rectangle is called the diameter.

4. The commutative property of multiplication is represented by $a \times b = b \times a$.

5. The formula to find the area of a circle is pi (3.14) times the diameter.

6. The formula to find the area of a triangle is ½ base times height.

7. The short word used for the number 3.142 is pi.

8. A dodecahedron is made up of 10 pentagons.

9. 11 x 11= 111

10. 22 x 15 = 225

11. 6 x 2.4 = 14.4

12. 13 x 71= 850

13. 63 ÷ 7 = 10.5

14. 200÷ 3 = 66.67

15. 1348 ÷ 2 = 674

16. 88 ÷ 10 = 8

17. 1 ½ + 2 ½ = 5

18. 13/36 is less than 2/3

19. 23/50 is greater than 2/3

20. 3 ¾ − 2/7 = 3.46 (or 3 13/28)

21. 8 8/10 = 8.8

22. 16 cups = 2 quarts

23. The area of a triangle with a base of 4 inches and a height of 2.4 inches is 4.8 inches.

24. The prime factors of 7 are 1, 3, and 7.

25. Rex baked 213 cookies, which is 19 more than Danielle baked. So, Danielle baked 194 cookies.

Reading ROOM

AWESOME VOCAB

1. What is the time and place of the action in a story called?

2. What are two or more words that are pronounced the same but have different meanings called?

3. What is the term for one or more letters added to the end of a root (base) word that changes the word's meaning?

4. Define the word "queasy."

5. What are the number of sound chunks in a word called?

a) Syllables
b) Plot
c) Noun

6. What is the "climax" of a story?

7. Define the word "coax."

8. What is the most common punctuation mark used to show separation of words or word groups within a sentence?

9. A short story that teaches a lesson is a:

   a) Simile

   b) Caption

   c) Fable

   d) Metaphor

10. What is a "bandit"?

11. What is a "simile"?

ANSWER KEY 6. The most exciting moment of the story turning point 7. persuade someone gradually or by flattery to do something 8. Comma 9. C 10. a robber or outlaw typically 11. A figure of speech comparing two things using "like" or "as." belonging to a gang

12. What is a "hyperbole"?

13. What is an "idiom"?

14. What is a "direct object"?

15. Define the word "obscure."

16. Which one of these words is an example of an adverb?

    a) Quickly

    b) Slow

    c) Home

    d) Flag

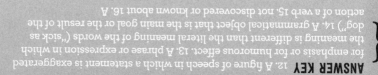

FAVORITE AUTHORS AND WRITERS

1. What famous poet wrote the poem "Autumn"?

2. Who wrote the famous lines:

"The Woods are lovely, dark and deep,
But I have promises to keep,
And miles to go before I sleep,
And miles to go before I sleep."
from a poem titled "Stopping by Woods on a Snowy Evening"?

3. Who wrote *The Cricket in Times Square*?

4. What was Mark Twain's real name?

a) James Mississppi

b) Roald Twain

c) Samuel Clemens

d) Mark Twice

5. Roald Dahl wrote which of the following books?

    a) The Witches

    b) Charlie and The Chocolate Factory

    c) Matilda

    d) all the above

6. Who wrote the book *Stargirl*?

7. What is the funny name of the author of *A Series of Unfortunate Events*?

8. Who wrote *Charlotte's Web*?

9. The author of *Flora & Ulysses* and *The Tale of Despereaux* has won the John Newbery Medal twice! What is her name?

10. Who wrote *The Secret Garden*?

BEST BOOKS EVER

11. What state does Sarah of *Sarah, Plain and Tall* come from?

a) Kansas

b) Alaska

c) Maine

d) Pennsylvania

12. Who are the main characters of *The Lighthouse Family: The Storm* by Cynthia Rylant?

13. In the story *Amos and Boris*, Amos is a _____ and Boris is a _____.

14. Match the book title with its main character(s).

1) Elmer Elevator   a) *The Fire Cat*

2) Pickles   b) *Top and Bottoms*

3) Isaac   c) *My Father's Dragon*

4) Bear and Hare   d) *The Treasure*

15. Where does the boy in *My Father's Dragon* run away to?

a) Narnia

b) Hogwarts

c) Wild Island

d) New York City

16. *The Song of Jellicles* by T.S. Eliot is about a....

a) Dog

b) Fish

c) Monkey

d) Cat

17. Where does *Bud, Not Buddy* take place?

  a) Austin, Texas

  b) Charlotte, North Carolina

  c) Kennebunkport, Maine

  d) Flint, Michigan

18. In *Bud, Not Buddy*, who does Bud set out to look for?

19. In *The Search for Delicious*, what is the main character Gaylan looking for?

  a) Candy

  b) A definition

  c) Friends

  d) Home

20. What is the name of the pig in *Charlotte's Web*?

21. In *Alice's Adventures in Wonderland*, the bottle that says "DRINK ME" makes her...

a) Fall asleep

b) Shrink

c) Fly

d) Become invisible

22. In *The Little Prince*, the young prince came to earth on . . .

a) An asteroid

b) A boat

c) A space ship

d) A plane

23. Who does Charlie bring with him on the tour of Wonka's Chocolate Factory?

24. In *Tuck Everlasting*, what secret power does the Tuck family possess?

25. What famous poem takes place in Mudville?

26. What does Carl Sandburg compare fog to in his poem "Fog"?

   a) A ghost

   b) A cat

   c) A person

   d) A cloud

27. *The Tale of Despereaux* is about a _____.

   a) Mouse

   b) Bat

   c) Elephant

   d) Snake

28. Who shows up in Harry's room and tells him not to return to Hogwarts in *Harry Potter and the Chamber of Secrets*?

   a) Voldemort

   b) Hagrid

   c) Ron

   d) Dobby

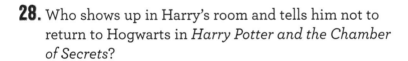

29. On what famous monument is the poem "The New Colossus" engraved?

30. In *The Hatchet,* how does Brain find himself abandoned in the wilderness?

31. What is the boy's name in The Black Stallion?

a) Billy

b) Alec

c) Sam

d) Stanley

32. In *Mr. Popper's Penguins,* what is Mr. Popper's occupation?

a) A salesman

b) An accountant

c) A painter

d) A teacher

33. In *James and the Giant Peach,* after his parents die, James is forced to go to _____.

    a) Live with his aunts

    b) A family friend's house

    c) An orphanage

34. The Pied Piper is from

    a) Hamelin

    b) London

    c) Boston

    d) New York

35. What does Laura call her parents in *Little House in the Big Woods*?

    a) Mother and Father

    b) Mom and Dad

    c) Mommy and Daddy

    d) Ma and Pa

36. In *The Stories Julian Tells*, what is Julian's little brother's name?

37. Where is the Cricket in *The Cricket in Times Square* from?

EXTRA CREDIT!

1. Match the book to the author:

1. *Ramona Quimby, Age 8*	a. Roald Dahl
2. *Tales of a Fourth Grade Nothing*	b. Louise Fitzhugh
3. *The Phantom Tollbooth*	c. Richard Atwater
4. *Mr. Popper's Penguins*	d. Judy Blume
5. *Walk Two Moons*	e. Beverly Cleary
6. *Harriet the Spy*	f. Sharon Creech
7. *Matilda*	g. Norton Juster
8. *The Giver*	h. Lois Lowry
9. *Bridge to Terabithia*	i. Katherine Paterson

2. Who wrote *The Hunger Games*?

a. Joan Collins

b. Phil Collins

c. Suzanne Collins

d. Tom Collins

3. What was unusual about how E.E. Cummings wrote his name?

4. Name the monkey ruler in *The Jungle Book*.

5. Complete the titles of these *Percy Jackson and the...* books:

a. ...*Lightning* _____

b. ...*Sea of* _____

c. ...*Titan's* _____

d. ...*Last* _____

e. ...*Battle of the* _____

ANSWER KEY 2. c 3. a lower case (e.e. cummings) 4. King Louie 5. a. *Thief* b. *Monsters* c. *Curse* d. *Olympian* e. *Labyrinth*

97

6. Is *The Giver* by Lois Lowry set in the future or the past?

7. In the *Frog and Toad* books, who is taller, Frog or Toad?

8. In Robert Browning's *The Pied Piper of Hamelin*, what does "pied" mean?

9. Complete the title of these children's classics:

a. *Chicka Chicka Boom* _____

b. *Brown Bear, Brown Bear, What Do You* _____?

c. *The Saggy, Baggy* _____

d. *Richard Scarry's Best* _____ *Ever*

e. *Blueberries for* _____

10. What sort of animal is the passive Ferdinand?

11. What surgery did *Madeline* need?

12. Where does *Madeline* take place?

13. Match the Hogwarts instructor to his or her subject.

1. Professor Binns   a. Care of Magical Creatures

2. Hagrid   b. Divination

3. Professor Snape   c. History of Magic

4. Professor Trelawney   d. Potions

14. What is the name of Harry's owl?

a. Arthur

b. Fezziwig

c. Hedwig

d. Ludwig

15. Which book came first, *Winnie-the-Pooh* or *The House on Pooh Corner*?

16. What was the last part of the Cheshire Cat to disappear?

17. Was *The Adventures of Huckleberry Finn* Mark Twain's first novel?

18. Did Charles Dickens write two sequels to *A Christmas Carol*?

19. What are the two cities in Charles Dickens' *A Tale of Two Cities*?

20. Meg, Jo, Beth and Amy all appear in what classic book by Louisa May Alcott?

21. The heavy metal band in the *Diary of a Wimpy Kid* books is called _____?

22. Which of the following is not used to describe Alex's day?

a. horrible

b. very bad

c. unbearable

d. no good

23. Which Chris Van Allsburg book came first, *Zathura* or *Jumanji*?

24. According to the Laura Numeroff book, a long chain of events will result *If You Give a Mouse a* _____.

25. Who is Waldo's dog in the *Where's Waldo* series?

a. Barky

b. Fido

c. Woof

d. Spider

26. Which of the following is not a *Where's Waldo?* book?

    a. *Where's Waldo? The Fantastic Journey*

    b. *Where's Waldo? The Wonder Book*

    c. *Where's Waldo? The Special Edition*

    d. *Where's Waldo? In Hollywood*

27. What is the Hardy Boys' home town?

    a. Ocean City

    b. Bayport

    c. Watercress

    d. Sea Breeze

TURN THE PAGE FOR A TRUE-OR-FALSE LIGHTNING ROUND!

HERE'S HOW TO GRADE A GROWN-UP:

0-5 QUESTIONS RIGHT: *Go Back to Second Grade!*

6-10 QUESTIONS RIGHT: *Nice Try... But Time to Repeat Grade Three!*

11-20 QUESTIONS RIGHT: *Lucky for you, Fourth Grade Wasn't So Bad—Back You Go!*

21+ QUESTIONS RIGHT: *Congratulations! You Might Be Ready for Middle School!*

READING ROOM: LIGHTNING ROUND!

1. Templeton is the name of the rat in *Charlotte's Web*.

2. The rabbit Alice meets has yellow fur.

3. "Who Has Seen the Wind" is a poem by Christina Rossetti.

4. The name of little boy in *The Cricket in Time Square* is Mario.

5. In *Bud, Not Buddy*, Bud's father is Herman E. Colloway.

6. Harry Potter is Voldemort's son.

7. A category of art, music, or literature is called genre.

8. *Sarah Plain and Tall* takes place in Kansas.

9. A "fallacy" is a false or misleading idea or notion.

10. Elmer Elevator is the main character of *The Treasure*.

11. In *Tuck Everlasting*, the man out to get the Tuck family wears a purple suit.

12. In *Tuck Everlasting*, Winnie ends up drinking from the spring.

13. "Figurative language" means language that goes beyond the literal meaning of words.

14. An "analogy" is a comparison of two different things that are similar in some way.

15. In *The Little Prince* the prince travels only to earth.

16. *Higgins, the Great* is about a boy named Mayo.

17. The evil principal in *Matilda* is named Miss Honey.

18. Pickles, from *The Fire Cat*, is a black cat.

19. Alice follows a rabbit down a rabbit hole, which ultimately brings her to Wonderland.

20. "Casey at the Bat" is about a tennis player.

21. Charlotte, in *Charlotte's Web*, is a spider.

22. In *Little Red Riding Hood and the Wolf* by Roald Dahl, Little Red Riding Hood shoots the wolf with a pistol.

23. *The Secret Garden* takes place in America.

24. *The Birchbark House*, by Louise Erdirch, is about a young girl living in the Ojibwa community

25. A folktale is a new story.

Lunch & RECESS

TASTY FOOD FACTS

1. George Washington Carver discovered more than 300 uses for what food?

2. One serving of what green leafy vegetable has more absorbable calcium than a small carton of milk?

3. What state produces the most maple syrup?

4. What state has the most crayfish?

5. Which state produces the most citrus fruit?

6. What Maine delicacy was once served to prisoners in colonial America?

7. Rhode Islanders are known to mix what with their milk?

8. What is the only U.S. state to grow coffee beans?

9. A New England-based coffee franchise says "America runs on" what?

10. On what New Orleans-centric holiday would you eat King's Cake?

11. In the Midwest, what dried white fish is soaked in a mixture of lye and water and served at holidays?

12. What do you call a Polish dumpling with a potato-cheese filling or a cabbage filling?

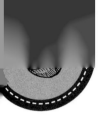

13. What Chinese-American chicken dish is named after a military leader?

14. What's the name of sushi made with crabmeat, avocado, and cucumber?

15. What Southern dish served on New Year's Day for good luck is a mix of black-eyed peas, chopped onions, and ham hock?

16. What American restaurant welcomes travelers with rocking chairs on porches?

17. What eating style is inspired by the way our hunter-gatherer ancestors ate?

18. What citrus fruit do science students use to convert chemical energy into electric power in a simple experiment?

ANSWER KEY 13. General Tso's chicken 14. California roll 15. Hoppin' John 16. Cracker Barrel 17. Paleo 18. lemon

19. What was the first food grown in space?

20. The laborers who built the Pyramids of Egypt were paid with which vegetables?

21. What vegetable is known in Italy as "crazy apple"?

22. What vegetable gets turned into a mode of transportation in "Cinderella"?

23. The world's most popular fruit is often mistaken as a vegetable. What is it?

24. What is the word for the study of fruits?

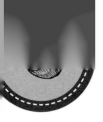

25. Match the mascot to the cereal:

1. Dig 'em Frog   a. Froot Loops

2. Toucan Sam   b. Rice Krispies

3. Snap, Crackle, and Pop   c. Frosted Flakes

4. Sugar Bear   d. Sugar Smacks

5. Tony the Tiger   e. Super Sugar Crisp

26. What is the Cocoa Puffs' Bird's name?

a. Kooky

b. Sonny

c. Socko

d. Wacko

27. What cereal is "Not for silly rabbits"?

28. What pirate is constantly trying to steal Cap'n Crunch?

29. Match the catchphrase to the fast food chain:

1. Where's the beef?	a. White Castle
2. Eat fresh	b. Burger King
3. What you crave	c. KFC
4. Home of the Whopper	d. Subway
5. Finger lickin' good	e. Wendy's
6. Think outside the bun	f. Taco Bell
7. I'm lovin' it	g. McDonald's

30. What color is the "way" in the Subway logo?

31. What color is the "Sub" in the Subway logo?

32. IHop's slogan is "Come hungry. Leave _____."

33. According to Mr. Owl, it takes how many licks to get to the center of a Tootsie pop?

34. Match the slogan to the candy:

1. Gimme a break
2. The Great American Chocolate Bar
3. Melts in your mouth, not in your hand
4. Sometimes you feel like a nut

a. *Almond Joy*
b. *Hershey's*
c. *Kit Kat*
d. *M&M's*

35. What candy bar consists of peanuts around a caramel center?

a. *Mr. Goodbar*
b. *Payday*
c. *Zagnut*
d. *Zero*

36. What do you get if you combine chocolate, marshmallows, and graham crackers?

37. What cream-filled cookies were first sold in 1912?

38. What Pennsylvania town is called "the sweetest place on earth"?

39. What do you call a tofu "turkey"?

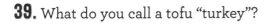

40. What do you call three birds in one—a turkey, a duck, and a chicken—served at Thanksgiving?

41. What do you call a combination of a croissant and a donut?

42. What expensive spice is the dried stamens of crocus flowers?

43. What vegetable is nicknamed "lady finger" and is used as a thickening agent in soups and stews?

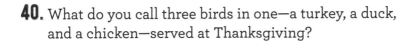

44. What tropical fruit has more lycopene than a tomato and is filled with black peppery seeds?

45. Who is the mayor of McDonaldland?

46. What is the core food at Famous Dave's?

a) Hamburgers
b) Chicken
c) Tacos
d) Barbecue

47. Which of the following has NOT been a Goldfish flavor?

a. BBQ
b. Sour Cream & Onion
c. French Toast
d. Mozzarella

48. What flavor of pie does Snow White bake in *Snow White and the Seven Dwarves*?

a. Apple
b. Gooseberry
c. Blackberry
d. Cherry

49. What candy was prominently featured in the movie *E.T.*?

50. What brand of bubble gum comes with a comic strip inside the wrapper?

51. What candy bar features a bee on the wrapper?

52. What chewing gum has frequently advertised itself using twins as models?

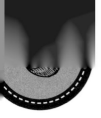

53. What animal is featured on Kid Cuisine advertisements and packaging?

54. In Apple Jacks commercials, what two characters race to the finish line (cereal bowl)?

55. How many chicken nuggets come in a MacDonald's kids meal?

56. In the movie *Ratatouille*, Remy is hunting for what in an old woman's house when he and his brother are spotted and shot at?

57. What food does Aladdin give to two small children in *Aladdin*?

58. What food does Pacha slurp down with a straw in the restaurant he eats at with Kuzco in *The Emperor's New Groove*?

59. What delectable treat does Big Daddy ask Tiana to whip up at the diner she works at in *The Princess and the Frog*?

61. What treat does the Abominable Snowman offer to Mike and Sully in *Monsters, Inc.*?

62. What steaming dish does Kronk prepare for Kuzco and Yzma's dinner in *The Emperor's New Groove*?

63. What food does Cogsworth instruct Beast to eat properly with a spoon in *Beauty and the Beast*?

64. What appetizer does the chef decide to make, to Sebastian's horror, in *The Little Mermaid*?

65. According to the sharks in *Finding Nemo*, what are fish, if not food?

66. In *Wall-E*, Wall-E's little cockroach friend jumps into what food that Wall-E puts out for him?

67. Food falls from the sky when a machine breaks down in what movie?

68. In the Christmas favorite, *Elf*, what does Buddy pack his stepmother for lunch?

69. According to Buddy in *Elf*, what do the elves say are the four main food groups?

70. In *Oliver and Company*, what food does Oliver help steal from a vendor?

71. What meal is Rapunzel's favorite in the Disney film *Tangled*?

72. What seafood restaurant gets its name from the movie *Forrest Gump*?

RECESS PROFESSIONAL

1. What type of jump roping uses more than one rope?

2. Glass blowers sometimes make what game pieces out of end-of-day leftover material?

3. What playground game started as a training exercise for Roman soldiers to improve their footwork?

4. What playground game involves a ball tied to the top of a 10-foot pole?

5. Miss Mary Mack was all dressed in what?

ANSWER KEY 72. Bubba Gump Shrimp Co. **1.** double Dutch **2.** marbles **3.** hopscotch **4.** tetherball **5.** black

123

6. "Miss Susie had a steamboat, the steamboat had a" what?

7. "Eeny, meeny, miny, moe, catch a tiger by the" what?

8. What Italian fortune-seeker from the 1200s traveled extensively, which may explain why children still use his name while playing hide-and-seek games?

9. Playing marbles is a basic introduction to what science of force and motion?

10. In marbles, what do you call the marble you shoot with?

11. In marbles, what do you call the target marbles you' aiming at?

12. What modern North American sport is a combination of two older sports—soccer and rugby?

13. What outdoor sport was invented in Chicago using a boxing glove, a stick, and a ball?

14. The leftfield wall in what park is known as "The Green Monster"?

  a. Coors Field

  b. Dodger Stadium

  c. Fenway Park

  d. Yankee Stadium

15. Who threw the only no-hitter in a World Series?

  a. Sandy Koufax

  b. Don Larsen

  c. Allie Reynolds

  d. Cy Young

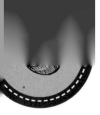

16. What team has won the most Super Bowls?

    a. Dallas Cowboys

    b. Oakland Raiders

    c. Pittsburgh Steelers

    d. San Francisco 49ers

17. What are the measurements of an NBA backboard?

    a. 6ft. by 3.5ft.

    b. 5ft. by 2.5ft.

    c. 5.5ft. by 3ft.

    d. 6.5ft. by 4 ft.

18. Is an official NBA basketball more or less than 30 inches in circumference?

19. Do goofy footers ride a skateboard with the left foot forward or the right foot?

20. How many red lines are there on a hockey rink?

21. How many inches tall is a bowling pin?

22. How much does a bowling pin weigh?

    a. 1-2 lbs
    b. 2-3 lbs
    c. 3-4 lbs
    d. 4-5 lbs

23. What is the distance in inches between the center of pin one and the center of pin 12?

24. What is a perfect score in bowling?

25. How many frames are in a game of bowling?

26. In what sport would an athlete land a double toe loop?

27. What sport is played on ice with brooms?

28. What sport is the modern verison of the Alongquin Indian game of stickball?

RAINY DAY GAMES

1. In what card game for four players is the goal to avoid winning sets of cards that include Hearts or the Queen of Spades?

2. What game piece is a flat, rectangular block with dots on it?

3. How many cards do you draw at the beginning of a basic game of Pokemon?

4. Which is not the color of an Uno card:

   a. Red

   b. Orange

   c. Green

   d. Blue

5. How many pairs of pants are in a game of Ants in the Pants?

6. How many monkeys do you need to hook together to win a game of Barrel of Monkeys?

7. What tells you how many spaces to move in Chutes and Ladders?

a. Dice

b. Tiles

c. A spinner

d. None of the above

8. How many pieces are there in a total Cootie?

9. How many buckets in a game of Hi Ho Cherry O?

10. How many blocks in a game of Jenga?

a. 48

b. 54

c. 62

d. 72

11. What is the highest number of dots on one standard Domino?

12. How many people can play Rock 'em Sock 'em Robots at one time?

13. In Rock 'em Sock 'em Robots, one robot is blue. What color is the other?

14. How many buttons are on each side of Rock 'em Sock 'em Robots?

15. What color is the boxing platform in Rock 'em Sock 'em Robots?

16. Does Dominoes primarily use cards or dice?

17. Are the players in Apples to Apples dealt green apple cards or red apple cards?

18. Are there more red or green cards in Apples to Apples?

19. How much time does it take for a Pictionary timer to run out?

20. What color Cranium spaces let players choose a category?

21. Which of the following is not a Cranium category?

a. Word Worm

b. Fact Junkie

c. Creative Cat

d. Star Performer

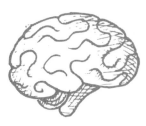

22. Which of the following objects is NOT part of the game Mouse Trap?

a. A bathtub

b. A bucket

c. A boot

d. An anvil

23. What does it say on a Mouse Trap space that would require a player to start operating the trap?

24. Which comes first in Mouse Trap, the diver or the marble?

25. In Clue, what is the name of the Colonel?

26. What color piece is Mrs. Peacock?

27. Which is NOT a room in Clue?

    a. Dining room

    b. Laundry room

    c. Kitchen

    d. Conservatory

28. In Clue, which player goes first?

    a. Mr. Green

    b. Col. Mustard

    c. Miss Scarlet

    d. Mrs. White

29. Which of these rooms does not have a secret passageway?

    a. Billiard room

    b. Conservatory

    c. Kitchen

    d. Study

30. How many spaces are there on a Monopoly board?

31. How much money do you get for passing "Go" in regular Monopoly?

32. What color are the $20 bills in Monopoly?

33. What color are the $1 bills in Monopoly?

34. How much money does each player start with in Monopoly?

35. Name the four Monopoly railroads.

36. What is the name of the Queen (later changed to a Princess) in Candy Land?

37. How many players can play Guess Who? at one time?

ANSWER KEY 33. Forty 31. $200 32. Blue 33. White 34. $1,500
35. Reading, B&O, Short Line, Pennsylvania
36. Queen Frostine 37. Two

38. In four square, is a ball that bounces on a line in or out?

39. In four square, do your feet have to stay in your square?

40. In hopscotch, does a marker that lands on a line count?

41. In chain tag, what happens to the "It" person after he or she tags someone?

42. In duck, duck, goose, do you get up and choose if you are tapped as a duck or if you are tapped as a goose?

43. In freeze tag, how do you get unfrozen?

44. How many holes in a standard wiffle ball?

45. What happens in dodge ball if you catch a ball thrown at you?

EXTRA CREDIT!

1. In competitive Four Square, are you allowed to spin the ball on a serve?

2. In Duck, Duck, Goose, do you get up and chase if you are tapped as a duck or if you are tapped as a goose?

3. In Freeze Tag, how do you get unfrozen?

4. How many games in a bocce match?

5. Kickball has been played since around...

    a. 1857

    b. 1917

    c. 1928

    d. 1954

6. How many points do you get in Cornhole for landing a bag on the platform?

7. How many points do you get in Cornhole for landing a bag in the hole?

8. What beats paper in Rock, Paper, Scissors?

9. In Wiffle Ball, what happens if a ball is caught while the ball is in motion in fair territory?

10. What happens in a standard game of croquet if your balls hit someone else's ball?

11. In ladder ball, which is worth three points, the top rung or the bottom rung?

TURN THE PAGE FOR A TRUE-OR-FALSE LIGHTNING ROUND!

HERE'S HOW TO GRADE A GROWN-UP:

0-5 QUESTIONS RIGHT: *Go Back to Second Grade!*

6-10 QUESTIONS RIGHT: *Nice Try... But Time to Repeat Grade Three!*

11-20 QUESTIONS RIGHT: *Lucky for you, Fourth Grade Wasn't So Bad—Back You Go!*

21+ QUESTIONS RIGHT: *Congratulations! You Might Be Ready for Middle School!*

LUNCH & RECESS LIGHTNING ROUND!

1. True or false: Snickers contains almonds.

2. True or False: Grape-Nuts contains neither grapes nor nuts.

3. True or false: The spaces in Chutes and Ladders are lettered.

4. True or false: In Clue, you may block a room to prevent another player from entering.

5. True or false: According to the rules of Monopoly, you collect money from the center of the board when you land on free parking.

6. True or false: In Monopoly, if you land on "Go" instead of passing it, you get $400, not $200.

ANSWER KEY 1. False—it contains peanuts **2.** True **3.** False, they're numbered **4.** True **5.** False **6.** False

7. Coca-Cola was first bottled in Mississippi.

8. New Jersey is known as the diner capital of the world.

9. A pescatarian is a person who eats a vegetarian diet that excludes meat, eggs, and dairy.

10. Bananas grow on trees.

11. Eat enough carrots and your skin will look orange.

12. A penguin is the mascot for Peanut Butter Crunch.

13. Cap'n Crunch's first name is Horatio.

14. Production of Twinkies stopped for several months in 2012 and 2013 due to bankruptcy proceedings.

15. Double Dutch is a type of jump roping that is done with an elastic band looped around two players' legs.

16. A traditional kickball ball is blue.

17. Peyton and Eli Manning are the only brothers to both be drafted with the #1 pick for the NFL.

18. A football field is 33 and 1/3 yards wide.

19. Rugby was first played with a soccer ball and a wooden peach basket.

20. The diameter of a basketball rim is 18 inches.

21. Darts is thought to have been invented by soldiers throwing arrows at the bottom of tree trunks and wooden casks.

22. Rock beats paper in Rock Paper Scissors.

23. A sun salutation is part of yoga.

24. Mod Podge is the term for Japanese paper folding.

25. Each player gets seven pawns in a game of Sorry!

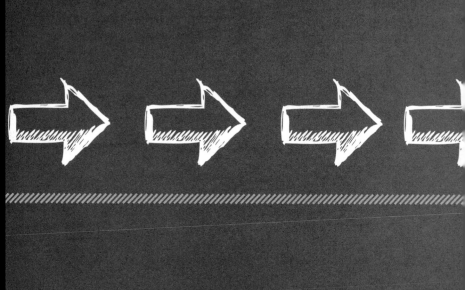

Around the WORLD

THE 50 NIFTY STATES

1. Match the state to its capital:

1. Alabama
2. Alaska
3. Arizona
4. Arkansas
5. California
6. Colorado
7. Connecticut
8. Delaware
9. Florida
10. Georgia
11. Hawaii
12. Idaho
13. Illinois
14. Indiana
15. Iowa
16. Kansas
17. Kentucky

18. Louisiana
19. Maine
20. Maryland
21. Massachusetts
22. Michigan
23. Minnesota
24. Mississippi
25. Missouri
26. Montana
27. Nebraska
28. Nevada
29. New Hampshire
30. New Jersey
31. New Mexico
32. New York
33. North Carolina
34. North Dakota

35. Ohio
36. Oklahoma
37. Oregon
38. Pennsylvania
39. Rhode Island
40. South Carolina
41. South Dakota
42. Tennessee
43. Texas
44. Utah
45. Vermont
46. Virginia
47. Washington
48. West Virginia
49. Wisconsin
50. Wyoming

a. Augusta

b. Providence

c. Frankfort

d. Springfield

e. Cheyenne

f. Columbus

g. Salem

h. Helena

i. Montgomery

j. Baton Rouge

k. Boston

l. Lansing

m. Boise

n. Harrisburg

o. Bismarck

p. Concord

q. Austin

r. Madison

s. Jackson

t. Pierre

u. Dover

v. Salt Lake City

w. Annapolis

x. Richmond

y. Honolulu

z. Oklahoma City

aa. Tallahassee

bb. Montpelier

cc. Topeka

dd. Olympia

ee. Saint Paul

ff. Raleigh

gg. Indianapolis

hh. Sacramento

ii. Atlanta

jj. Little Rock

kk. Santa Fe

ll. Lincoln

mm. Jefferson City

nn. Des Moines

oo. Denver

pp. Phoenix

qq. Hartford

rr. Carson City

ss. Albany

tt. Juneau

uu. Trenton

vv. Nashville

ww. Columbia

xx. Charleston

kk: 32. ss: 33. ff: 34. o: 35. f: 36. z: 37. gg: 38. nn: 39. b: 40. ww: 41. t: 42. vv: 43. q: 44. v: 45. bb: 46. x: 47. dd: 48. xx: 49. r: 50. e

147

2. Which of the five New England states was not the name of one of the original 13 colonies?

3. Which of the 13 original colonies was farthest south?

4. What state has the smallest amount of land?

5. What state has the largest amount of land?

6. What state boasts the tallest sea mountain in the world?

7. What is the highest mountain in North America?

8. What state has the most miles of coastline?

9. In which state is Old Faithful?

10. What is the largest freshwater lake in the world?

11. What state has the country's only active diamond mine?

12. What state is at the geographic center of North America?

13. Which state has the most people?

14. In Washington, D.C., what does the "D.C." stand for?

15. In which state is Arches National Park?

16. In which state is Crater Lake National Park?

ANSWER KEY 10. Lake Superior 11. Arkansas 12. North Dakota 13. California 14. District of Columbia 15. Utah 16. Oregon

149

17. In which state is Great Sand Dunes National Park?

18. In which state is Mammoth Cave National Park?

19. In which state is Acadia National Park?

20. In which state is Shenandoah National Park?

21. In which state is Mount Rainier?

HISTORY, NEAR AND FAR!

1. What are the first ten amendments of the Constitution of the United States known as?

2. What are the first ten amendments of the Constitution?

3. Name the three branches of our government.

4. What branch of government do the senators of each state belong to?

5. What branch does the American court system belong to?

6. What amendment made all former slaves U.S. citizens and laid the foundation for the Civil Rights Movement?

7. How many justices are on the Supreme Court?

ANSWER KEY 2. The freedom of speech, the right to bear arms, the restriction against quartering soldiers in private homes without consent of the homeowners, the right against unreasonable search and seizure of private materials in a private home, the right to a fair trial, the right to a speedy and public trial, the right to a trial by jury, the right against excessive bails or fines (also the right against cruel and unusual punishment), the right to an individual's natural rights, and the right to powers not specifically delegated to the government in the Constitution. 3. the Executive Branch, the Legislative Branch, and the Judicial Branch. 4. the Legislative Branch 5. the Judicial Branch 6. the Fourteenth Amendment 7. nine

151

8. What was the first currency introduced in the United States?

9. What is the average life span of an American dollar bill?

10. What colors in the background of the 2003 $20 bill?

11. Who is on the front of the $10 bill?

12. The lyrics for "This Land Is My Land" go from the Redwood Forest to where?

13. Yankee Doodle stuck a feather in his cap and called it what?

14. In "My Country, 'Tis of Thee," we sing of "land where my fathers died" and "land of the pilgrims'" what?

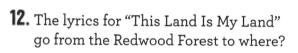

15. In "America the Beautiful," we sing of "amber waves of" what?

16. In "You're a Grand Old Flag," we sing of "the home of the free and the" what?

17. In what year did Columbus make the first of four trips to the Caribbean on Spanish ships named the *Niña*, the *Pinta*, and the *Santa Maria*?

18. Who was the first to sign the Declaration of Independence?

19. Who was the primary author of the Declaration of Independence?

20. What man is known for riding through the night, announcing the British army's advance toward Lexington and Concord?

21. Who is known for creating the first American flag for General George Washington?

22. Whose face is on the $100 bill?

23. During the time that the Constitution was written, how much of a "person" was an African American or slave "worth"?

24. Who was the 2nd president of the United States?

25. Who was the 16th president of the United States?

26. Who was the principal author of the Constitution of the United States?

27. In what year was Jamestown established as the first permanent English colony in the New World?

28. What Indian Princess was kidnapped by colonists and married one of them, marking the beginning of eight years of peace between the English and the Powhatan people?

29. Before the Pilgrims stepped off the *Mayflower*, the men signed what statement?

30. Who was banished from Massachusetts Bay colony and started a colony based on the idea of separation of church and state?

31. Pennsylvania became a refuge for people of what religion who would not give their loyalty to any king?

32. Which American colony became a refuge for Catholics?

ANSWER KEY 28. Pocahontas 29. the Mayflower Compact 30. Roger Williams 31. the Quakers (or Society of Friends) 32. Maryland

155

33. American colonists were upset when King George III raised taxes to pay for what war?

34. In 1770, violence broke out in Boston between American colonists and British soldiers with five colonists being killed. What do we call this event?

35. What do we call the series of laws passed by British Parliament to punish colonists for dumping tea in Boston harbor?

36. What organization was founded by Samuel Adams?

37. What enslaved woman's lawsuit in 1781 would lead to the abolition of slavery in Massachusetts?

38. What American colonist is famous for writing "Common Sense," a pamphlet that encouraged rebellion against British rule?

39. Who is best known for being a traitor during the Revolutionary War, defecting to the British and plotting the surrender of American troops?

40. What American colonist argued the case for resisting the British with the words "give me liberty or give me death"?

41. The Second Continental Congress met in 1775 with delegates from the 13 colonies coming together to choose a general to lead them against the British. Who did they choose?

42. On July 4, 1776, the Second Continental Congress signed what document?

43. What song did Francis Scott Key write after witnessing the British bombardment of Fort McHenry?

44. In what year did the Louisiana Purchase take place?

45. What expedition brought back a dinosaur skull, which President Thomas Jefferson displayed at Monticello?

46. What war gave the U.S. confidence to write the Monroe Doctrine, warning Europeans not to try to colonize the Americas?

47. In the 1820 Missouri Compromise, Maine entered the Union as a free state, and what state entered as a slave state?

48. Name four of the eight presidents who died in office.

49. Of the eight presidents who died while president, which were assassinated?

50. Who took over as president after Abraham Lincoln's death?

51. Who was president during the Radical Reconstruction that followed the Civil War?

52. What president is said to have gotten stuck in the White House bathtub due to his size?

53. Amelia Bloomer believed in equal rights for women and is known for inventing what?

54. During the Civil War, what general surrendered to General Ulysses S. Grant?

ANSWER KEY 49. Abraham Lincoln, James A. Garfield, William McKinley, and John F. Kennedy 50. Andrew Johnson 51. Andrew Johnson 52. William H. Taft 53. bloomers (or pants that women wore under skirts) 54. General Robert E. Lee

159

55. What man led the Rough Riders in defeating the Spanish at the Battle of San Juan Hill before he became a U.S. president?

56. What event started the Great Depression?

57. What do we call President Lincoln's speech that began with "Fourscore and seven years ago..."?

58. What was the name of the unofficial boundary between the North and the South?

59. What happened on December 7, 1942 that led to the U.S. joining the Allies in World War II?

60. What's the predominate Native American tribe in Alaska?

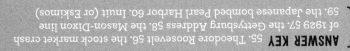

61. What Native American tribe built the cliff dwellings in Colorado?

62. When we study the European Middle Ages, what do we call the way of living in which people received land in exchange for serving masters or lords?

63. In 1066, William the Conquerer was crowned king of what country?

64. What document signed in 1215 sets forth the idea that there is a common law that all people must follow?

65. What teenage girl successfully headed a French army in 1429 before being burned at the stake?

66. King Charles of Spain sent what Portuguese seaman on what ended up being the first trip around the world?

67. Who began the Protestant Reformation by printing the Ninety-five Theses?

68. Who invented the printing press around 1440?

GLOBETROTTER GEOGRAPHY

1. On a world map, the lines that run from pole to pole are called meridians. What do we call the lines that run parallel to the equator?

2. What do we call a narrow strip of land connecting two larger areas of land?

3. What is a fan-shaped deposit of mud and sand at the mouth of a river?

4. What imaginary line runs from the North Pole to the South Pole, passing through Greenwich, England?

5. What sort of map best shows elevation?

6. Which of the Seven Wonders of the Ancient World do tourists still visit in Egypt?

7. The world's first civilizations were built near rivers. What early civilization was between the Tigris and the Euphrates?

8. The Phoenicians improved upon cuneiform, creating what?

9. What ancient Greek wrote *The Iliad* and *The Odyssey*?

10. What Italian city was buried under hot ash when Mount Vesuvius erupted?

11. What's the former name of the city we call Istanbul?

12. A Byzantine emperor codified legal ideas saying that a person is innocent until proven guilty and no one should be punished for what they think. What is this set of laws called?

13. What red-haired Viking discovered Greenland?

14. What explorer in search of cities of gold led an expedition into the area we now call Arizona and New Mexico?

15. What ancient civilization built palaces and temples in the jungles of Guatemala?

16. Who built Machu Picchu?

17. What is the longest river in Europe?

18. What Canadian Province used to be called New France?

19. Muslims pray facing what city where Muhammad was born?

20. What world religion was born in the Indus River Valley in India?

21. Dutch people come from what country?

22. Danish people came from what country?

EXTRA CREDIT!

1. Do even numbered highways go east-west or north-south?

2. Is a low numbered route more likely to be in the south or north?

3. Match the city to the river it is located next to:

1 Cincinnati   a. Danube

2. Dusseldorf   b. Rhine

3. Yonkers   c. Ohio

4. Vienna   d. Hudson

4. Is it longer to drive from Kansas City to Chicago or from Washington, D.C. to New York City?

5. What is the oldest city in the USA?

   a. Boston

   b. Charleston, S.C.

   c. Philadelphia

   d. St. Petersburg, Fla.

6. In what city would you find the Gateway Arch?

7. How large is New York's Central Park?

   a. 343 acres

   b. 563 acres

   c. 614 acres

   d. 843 acres

8. A Statue of Liberty pass also gets you admission to...

   a. New Jersey

   b. Ellis Island

   c. The Empire State Building

   d. The Tenement Museum

9. In what D.C. neighborhood is the Supreme Court located?

   a. Capitol Hill

   b. Adams Morgan

   c. Dupont Circle

   d. Cleveland Park

10. Does the White House have a public rest room?

11. Which has a longer shoreline: Maryland or New Jersey?

12. Which is not a river in Iowa:

   a. Raccoon River

   b. Des Moines River

   c. Wapsipinicon River

   d. Hullabaloo River

13. Is free Wi-Fi available on the Washington Mall?

14. What state has adopted this motto: "Eureka!"

15. What state has adopted this motto: "North to the future"?

16. What state has adopted this motto: "The crossroads of America"?

17. What state has adopted this motto: "Our liberties we prize and our rights we maintain"?

18. What state has adopted this motto: "Live free or die"?

19. What state has adopted this motto: "Hope"?

20. What state has adopted this motto: "Liberty and prosperity"?

21. What state has adopted this motto: "All for our country"?

22. What state has adopted this motto: "Let the welfare of the people be the supreme law"?

23. What state has adopted this motto: "Union, justice, confidence"?

24. Who controlled most of the world in 500 BCE?

    a. Romans

    b. Persians

    c. Aztecs

    d. Greeks

25. The Buddha was originally a prince named...

    a. Siddhartha

    b. Silmmarion

    c. Sidvicious

    d. Siddeus

26. In England, which was built first: Westminster Abbey or The Tower of London?

27. Which of Columbus's ships sank?

    a. Nina

    b. Pinta

    c. Santa Maria

    d. None of them

28. How many voyages did Columbus make to the New World?

    a. 1

    b. 2

    c. 3

    d. 4

29. The Eastern Roman Empire was also referred to by what name now used to mean "complex and confusing"?

    a. Byzantine

    b. Labyrinthine

    c. Praetorian

    d. Prolix

30. The Black Death was actually what disease?

    a. Bubonic plague

    b. Diphtheria

    c. Ebola virus

    d. Smallpox

31. What was Louis XIV's nickname?

  a. The Bald King

  b. The Golden King

  c. The Little King

  d. The Sun King

32. What term was given to the persecution, torture, and occasional execution of those who denied the authority of the church?

33. Although Christopher Columbus was Italian, what country financed his expedition to the new world?

34. What were the British coming to do when Paul Revere warned that they were on the way?

  a. arrest Samuel Adams and John Hancock

  b. burn Boston

  c. confiscate colonists' horses

  d. take over an armory

35. Benjamin Franklin was ambassador to what country?

36. George Washington and Thomas Jefferson both married wealthy widows named _____.

37. Who wrote the first 10 amendments to the Bill of Rights?

a. Madison

b. Hamilton

c. Jefferson

d. Franklin

38. Who was the first vice president?

a. John Adams

b. John Quincy Adams

c. Aaron Burr

d. Thomas Jefferson

39. When was the last signature on the Declaration of Independence added?

40. Match the colony to its founder:

1. Connecticut   a. Cecilius Calvert

2. Georgia   b. Thomas Hooker

3. Maryland   c. James Oglethorpe

4. Rhode Island   d. Roger Williams

41. What was the first battle of the Revolutionary War?

a. Boston Massacre

b. Bunker Hill

c. Lexington and Concord

d. Yarmouth

42. What nickname is sometimes given to the Battle of Lexington and Concord?

    a. The Cold War

    b. The Mother of All Battles

    c. The Shot Heard 'Round the World

    d. The World Turned Upside Down

43. What did Paul Revere do for a living?

    a. Blacksmith

    b. Horse breeder

    c. Minister

    d. Silversmith

44. In what city was George Washington inaugurated?

    a. Boston

    b. New York

    c. Philadelphia

    d. Washington

45. Match the Revolutionary-era quote to the speaker credited with saying it:

1. Don't fire until you see the whites of their eyes.
2. Give me liberty or give me death.
3. I have not yet begun to fight.
4. I only regret that I have but one life to give for my country.
5. These are the times that try men's souls.

a. Nathan Hale
b. Patrick Henry
c. John Paul Jones
d. Thomas Paine
e. William Prescott

46. Article I of the Constitution deals with:

a. Elections
b. The executive branch
c. The judicial branch
d. The legislative branch

47. Who was president of the Continental Congress in 1776?

48. Who was president of the Constitutional Convention?

  a. John Hancock

  b. Thomas Jefferson

  c. James Madison

  d. George Washington

49. The Third Amendment, seldom used today but of great concern to the newly independent colonists, bans the government from forcing you to:

  a. grow crops

  b. house troops

  c. pay poll taxes

  d. swear a loyalty oath

50. What was the first southern state to secede from the Union?

51. Match the Civil War battle to the state in which it took place.

1. Antietam
2. Bull Run
3. Chickamauga
4. Gettysburg
5. Shiloh
6. Vicksburg

a. Georgia
b. Maryland
c. Mississippi
d. Pennsylvania
e. Tennessee
f. Virginia

52. A compromise at the Constitutional Convention counted slaves as how many people?

a. 0
b. ½
c. ⅗
d. 1

53. Match the state to the country that controlled it before the U.S.:

1. Alaska   a. France

2. Florida   b. Mexico

3. Louisiana   c. Russia

4. Texas   d. Spain

54. Match the works to their authors:

1. Common Sense   a. Ben Franklin

2. Declaration of Independence   b. Alexander Hamilton, John Jay, James Madison

3. The Federalist Papers

4. Poor Richard's Almanack   c. Thomas Jefferson

5. The Wealth of Nations   d. Thomas Paine

     e. Adam Smith

55. What Delaware patriot, dying of cancer, rode back to the Continental Congress on horseback to cast his vote for independence?

a. Robert Dover

b. Thomas McKean

c. George Read

d. Caesar Rodney

56. Who was the defense attorney for the British soldiers blamed for the Boston Massacre?

a. John Adams

b. Lord Cornwallis

c. Thomas Jefferson

d. William Pitt

57. Did Bill Tonelli sign the Declaration of Independence?

58. Before the Constitution, what was America governed by?

59. What battle ended the Revolutionary War?

a. Saratoga

b. Ticonderoga

c. Trenton

d. Yorktown

60. What French nobleman visited America in 1831, and assessed the new country in his book "Democracy in America"?

a. Jacques Barzun

b. Alexis de Tocqueville

c. Jean Lafitte

d. Jean Rimbaud

61. How high at most places is the Great Wall of China?

    a. 8 ft.

    b. 12 ft.

    c. 18 ft.

    d. 25 ft

62. What title is Prince Charles' wife Camilla known by?

    a. Duchess of Cornwall

    b. Duchess of Hempstead

    c. Duchess of Middleton

    d. She has no title

AROUND THE WORLD: LIGHTNING ROUND!

1. True or false: Benjamin Franklin was the fourth president of the United States.

2. American soldiers forced the Cherokee to walk 800 miles.

3. Francis is the most common name for popes.

4. There are 200 Senators in Congress.

5. There are 435 Representatives in the House of Representatives.

6. The Constitution of the United States was written in Washington, D.C.

7. Jamestown was named for King James I of England.

8. New York City was originally called New Netherland.

9. The Treaty of Paris formally ended the Revolutionary War.

10. "Fourscore and seven years" means 47 years.

11. Abraham Lincoln was assassinated less than a week after the end of the Civil War.

12. John F. Kennedy was also a former film star.

13. A strait is a narrow body of water connecting two larger bodies of water.

14. The common abbreviation a.m. stands for "ante meridiem."

15. New Hampshire has the country's most eastern location.

16. Alaska has the country's most western location.

17. The Boston Protest Party is the name of the protest in which American colonists dumped 92,000 pounds of tea into Boston harbor.

18. Yosemite National Park is located in Montana.

19. Benjamin Franklin is on the front of the $100 bill.

20. You must be 45 years old in order to run for President.

ANSWER KEY 14. True 15. False—it's Maine 16. True 17. False—it's the Boston Tea Party 18. False 19. True 20. False

21. Franklin D. Roosevelt said, "Speak softly and carry a big stick."

22. The Pilgrims settled Plymouth in 1620.

23. In "Home on the Range," we sing that "the deer and the antelope" dance.

24. In "God Bless America," we sing "from the mountains, to the prairies, to the oceans white with foam."

25. Jimmy Carter was a peanut farmer before running for president.

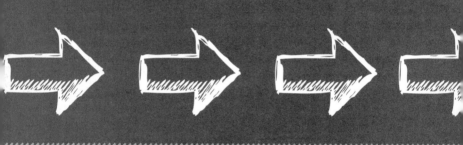

After-School
ACTIVITIES

GAMING AND COMICS

1. What two colors are the arrow footpads on a standard Dance Dance Revolution arcade game?

2. What color is Pac-Man?

3. What does a white bird drop in Angry Birds?

4. In Angry Birds, what is a player trying to hit with the birds?

5. How many smaller birds can the blue bird separate into in Angry Birds?

6. DC or Marvel?:

1. Spiderman
2. Wonder Woman
3. Super-Man
4. The Hulk
5. Batman
6. Fantastic Four

7. What superpower does Mr. Fantastic have?

8. Match the comic book hero to his secret identity:

1. Bruce Banner	a. The Incredible Hulk
2. Clark Kent	b. Super-Man
3. Peter Parker	c. Spiderman
4. Tony Stark	d. Iron man
5. Bruce Wayne	e. Batman
6. James "Logan" Howlett	f. Wolverine
7. Steve Rogers	g. Captain America

ANSWER KEY 6. 1. *Marvel* 2. *DC* 3. *DC* 4. *Marvel* 5. *DC* 6. *Marvel* 7. He can stretch his body 8. 1. The Incredible Hulk; 2. Super-Man; 3. Spiderman; 4. Iron man; 5. Batman; 6. Wolverine; 7. Captain Americ

191

9. Name each villain's nemesis:

1. Loki

2. Magneto

3. Dr. Octopus

4. Deathstroke

5. The Shredder

10. What is Garfield's owner's dog's name?

11. What is Garfield's favorite food?

12. What is the relationship between Peanuts characters Linus and Lucy?

13. Who is older, Charlie Brown or Sally Brown?

14. What is Lucy's last name?

15. What is Linus' younger brother's name?

16. What does Peppermint Patty call Charlie Brown?

17. What color is Schroeder's hair?

18. Who is in love with Schroeder?

19. What does Marcy usually call Charlie Brown?

20. What color hair does the girl who Charlie Brown has a crush on have?

21. Does Snoopy play on Charlie Brown's baseball team?

22. Who is Snoopy's enemy when he is fantasizing about being the World War I Flying Ace?

23. What is Snoopy's nickname when he is wearing sunglasses?

24. Is Charlie Brown bald?

25. How much does Lucy traditionally charge for psychiatric help?

26. Does Pig-Pen play an instrument in *A Charlie Brown Christmas*?

27. What is Linus' teacher's name?

   a. Miss Omar

   b. Miss Othmar

   c. Miss Rothmear

   d. Miss Rothenmeier

28. Lucy's dress is usually what color?

29. What position does Lucy usually play on the Peanuts baseball team?

CELEBS, TV, MOVIES, AND MUSIC

1. Are actresses Julia and Emma Roberts related?

2. Stefani Germanotta is better known as whom?

3. Who was known as Honest Abe?

4. Katy Perry was married to what comic actor:

    a. Russell Brand
    b. Jim Carrey
    c. Steve Coogan
    d. Ricky Gervais

5. The band One Direction was originally made up of five boys. What were their names?

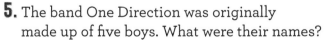

ANSWER KEY 29. Right field (sometimes center field) 1. Yes 2. Lady Gaga 3. Abraham Lincoln 4. a 5. Niall Horan, Zayn Malik, Liam Payne, Harry Styles, and Louis Tomlinson

195

6. Finish the song title:

1. " I Really ____" by Carly Rae Jepsen

2. "One Last ___" by Ariana Grande

3. "Love Me ___" by Ellie Goulding

4. "Uptown ___" by Mark Ronson feat. Bruno Mars

5. "Thinking ___" by Ed Sheeran

6. "Shut Up ___" by Walk the Moon

7. "Dear _____" by Meghan Trainor

8. "Honey ____" by Andy Grammer

9. "I'm ___" by Jason Mraz

10. "I'm Not ___" by Sam Smith

11. "Counting ___" by One Republic

12. "This Girl ___" by Alicia Keys

13. "You Belong ___" by Taylor Swift

14. "Hot ___" by Katy Perry

15. "A Sky ___" by Coldplay

16. "Play ___" by Luke Bryan

17. "She Looks ___" by Five Seconds of Summer

18. "Stay ___" by Zedd

19. "Adore ___" by Miley Cyrus

20. "Burnin' ___" by Jason Aldean

ANSWER KEY 6. 1. Like You, 2. Time, 3. Like You Do, 4. Funk, 5. Out Loud, 6. And Dance, 7. Future Husband, 8. I'm Good 9. Yours, 10. The Only One, 11. Stars, 12. Is On Fire, 13. With Me, 14. n Cold, 15. Full of Stars, 16. It Again, 17. So Perfect, 18. The Night, 19. You, 20. It Down

7. Who became famous after performing the hit song "Royals"?

8. What or whom does Lady Gaga claim she will marry in her 2011 hit song, "Marry _____"?

9. In "The 12 Days of Christmas," what is given on the sixth day?

10. In "The 12 Days of Christmas," what is given on the eighth day?

11. In "The 12 Days of Christmas," what is given on the eleventh day?

12. What number reindeer is Rudolph?

13. In "This Land is Your Land," the singer saw the endless skyway above. What was seen below?

ANSWER KEY 7. Lorde 8. The Night 9. Geese-a-laying 10. Maids-a-milking 11. Pipers piping 12. Nine 13. "that golden valley."

197

14. How many octaves are there on a typical upright piano?

15. How many keys are there in an octave?

16. What is a piano chord?

17. What hand are treble clef notes played with?

18. What kinds of notes are played with the black keys on a piano?

19. What is the end (non-playing) piece of a clarinet called?

20. What is the main difference between a typical Western flute and a recorder?

21. How many playing holes are there on a typical Western flute?

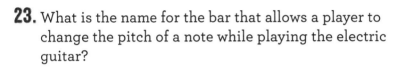

22. What are the metal "strips" that run horizontally across the neck of a guitar called?

23. What is the name for the bar that allows a player to change the pitch of a note while playing the electric guitar?

24. Which sound does the snare drum provide: a crisp, high-pitched sound, or a deep, soft sound?

25. In a drum kit, what is the hi-hat?

26. Which is not a type of drum

    a. The Hang drum

    b. The Jug drum

    c. The Talking drum

    d. The Finch drum

ANSWER KEY 21. sixteen 22. Frets 23. The whammy bar 24. A crisp, high-pitched sound 25. A set of two cymbals played by pressing a foot pedal, which brings the cymbals together 26. d

199

27. What is Arthur the Aardvark's last name?

28. What is the name of the teacher on *The Magic School Bus*?

29. The mean farmers in *The Fantastic Mr. Fox* are Boggis, Bunce, and _____

a. Bligh

b. Bean

c. Bunch

d. Blech

30. Match the movie to the opposing team:

1. *The Mighty Ducks*   a. Team Iceland

2. *D2: The Mighty Ducks*   b. The Hawks

3. *D3: The Mighty Ducks*   c. The Varsity Warriors

31. What is the name of the girl who plays on the Mighty Ducks team in all three films?

a. Carol

b. Connie

c. Catherine

d. Cynthia

32. Complete the names of these Hayao Miyazaki animated films:

1. Howl's Moving _____

2. Spirited _____

3. _____ Mononoke

4. Kiki's Delivery _____

5. My _____ Totoro

6. _____ in the Sky

33. What fuel is manufactured by Monsters, Inc.?

34. What is Mr. Incredible's occupation when not working as a superhero?

a. Advertising executive

b. Cook

c. Insurance adjuster

d. Truck driver

35. What is the name of the main villain in *The Incredibles*?

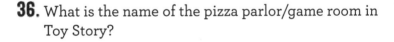

a. Flattop

b. Frozone

c. Mr. Glass

d. Syndrome

36. What is the name of the pizza parlor/game room in Toy Story?

37. What is Sid's last name in *Toy Story*?

    a. Johnson

    b. Philips

    c. Davis

    d. Lasseter

38. What is the name of Woody's horse in *Toy Story 2* and *Toy Story 3*?

39. What is WALL-E's favorite musical?

    a. *Cats*

    b. *Fiddler on the Roof*

    c. *Hello, Dolly!*

    d. *Singin' in the Rain*

40. In what small town does most of the action take place in *Cars*?

41. Which model of car is NOT among the "lemons" trying to destroy the racecars in *Cars 2*?

    a. Gremlin

    b. Pacer

    c. Pinto

    d. Yugo

42. In *Beauty and the Beast*, what is Belle's father's invention supposed to do?

43. What is Gaston "especially good at"?

44. In *Beauty and the Beast*, the rose was enchanted to bloom until the Prince's _____ birthday.

45. Who says the Prince in *The Little Mermaid* looks "kinda hairy and slobbery"?

46. For how many days does the potion turn Ariel into a human?

47. What exactly is the thing that gets called a "dinglehopper"?

48. What is the name of the human that Ursula transforms into?

49. What is the name of the mouse in *Dumbo*?

50. In the Disney film, which hand of Captain Hook's is a hook, left or right?

51. What are Lady and Tramp eating when "Bella Notte" is sung to them?

52. In *The Fox and the Hound*, is Copper the fox or the hound?

53. How many kittens star in *The Aristocats*?

54. What is the hero's name in *Tangled*?

  a. Flint Riser

  b. Flynn Rider

  c. Frank Rymen

  d. Fred Reisler

55. Which of the following is not a character in *Brother Bear*?

  a. Koda

  b. Kenai

  c. Sitka

  d. Sakina

56. Who is the father of Hercules?

57. What are the names of the two evil minions of Hades in *Hercules*?

    a. Pain and Pleasure

    b. Pain and Panic

    c. Mean and Nasty

    d. Hurt and Help

58. Which song came earlier in Disney's *The Hunchback of Notre Dame*: "God Help the Outcasts" or "A Guy Like You"?

59. What kind of animals are the Rescuers?

60. Match the villain to the movie:

1. Cruella de Vil	a. *101 Dalmatians*
2. Dr. Facilier	b. *Aladdin*
3. Frollo	c. *Bambi*
4. Gaston	d. *Beauty and the Beast*
5. Hades	e. *The Great Mouse Detective*
6. Jafar	f. *Hercules*
7. Madame Medusa	g. *The Hunchback of Notre Dam*
8. Maleficent	h. *The Jungle Book*
9. Man	i. *The Lion King*
10. Ratcliffe	j. *The Little Mermaid*
11. Professor Ratigan	k. *Mulan*
12. Scar	l. *Oliver and Company*
13. Shan Yu	m. *Pinocchio*
14. Shere Khan	n. *Pocahontas*
15. Stromboli	o. *The Princess and the Frog*
16. Sykes	p. *The Rescuers*
17. Ursula	q. *Sleeping Beauty*

ANSWER KEY 60. 1. a; 2. o; 3. g; 4. d; 5. f; 6. b; 7. p; 8. q; 9. c; 10. n; 11. e; 12. i; 13. k; 14. h; 15. m; 16. l; 17. j.}

61. What does Wendy sew back to Peter Pan?

62. What is the name of the Lion King at the beginning of the movie?

63. What is Sleeping Beauty's real name?

64. In the Disney version of *Robin Hood*, what kind of animal is Robin Hood?

65. Match the supporting characters in the Disney *Robin Hood* to the animal:

1. Allan-a-Dale	a. Badger
2. Friar Tuck	b. Bear
3. Little John	c. Lion
4. Prince John	d. Rooster
5. Sheriff of Nottingham	e. Wolf

66. Which was part of *The Three Caballeros*: Donald Duck or Mickey Mouse?

67. What is the mother cat's name in *The Aristocats*?

a. Duchess

b. Dainty

c. Daliah

d. Dorcett

68. Which of the following Disney princesses was not a princess by birth:

a. Snow White

b. Belle

c. Jasmine

d. Aurora

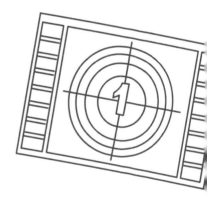

69. Which Disney princess never technically became a princess by bloodline or marriage?

    a. Mulan

    b. Ariel

    c. Pocahontas

    d. Belle

70. Which Disney princess has a tiger as a sidekick?

71. Which Disney princess has mice as sidekicks?

72. What is Belle's father's name?

    a. Mitchell

    b. Michael

    c. Maurice

    d. Maury

73. Which Disney princess has the most siblings?

    a. Cinderella

    b. Jasmine

    c. Ariel

    d. Mulan

74. Which Disney princess sings "the way you did once upon a dream"?

75. Which Disney princess do we see as a baby:

    a. Cinderella

    b. Snow White

    c. Aurora

    d. Jasmine

76. Where does *The Princess and the Frog* primarily take place?

77. In *The Princess and the Frog*, where is Prince Naveen from?

    a. Caldonia

    b. Maldonia

    c. Cardonia

    d. Freedonia

78. In *The Princess and the Frog*, what is Dr. Facilier also known as?

    a. The Shadow Man

    b. Lord of Darkness

    c. Beast of the Moon

    d. The Man from Beyond

79. Who is Porky Pig's girlfriend?

80. What instrument does cartoon character Angus McCrory play?

81. What is the name of Marvin the Martian's hairy friend?

    a. Hughie

    b. Hugo

    c. Gossamer

    d. Hungry-O

82. What color are Bugs Bunny's gloves?

83. *Anastasia* concerns what country's royal family?

84. The prologue song in *Anastasia* is "Once Upon a _____."

85. What fairy tale ballet do the characters in *Anastasia* attend?

86. In *The Prince of Egypt*, is Moses adopted by the Pharaoh's daughter or by his wife?

87. Which is not a song in *The Prince of Egypt*:

a. "Through Heaven's Eyes"

b. "Pharaoh's Dream"

c. "Playing with the Big Boys"

d. "The Plagues"

88. How many orphan dinosaurs make the trek in *The Land Before Time*?

89. What kind of dinosaur are the longnecks?

a. Stegosaurus

b. Apatosaurus

c. Saurolophus

d. Triceratops

90. What does NIMH in *The Secret of Nimh* stand for?

91. What is Fievel and his family's last name in *An American Tail*?

92. What does Fievel think there are none of in America?

93. What kind of animal is king in *All Dogs Go to Heaven*?

94. What kind of dog is Charlie in *All Dogs Go to Heaven*?

95. What animal is the human boy Edmond transformed into in *Rock-a-Doodle*?

    a. A cow

    b. A cat

    c. A duck

    d. A pig

96. What is the name of the rooster in *Rock-a-Doodle*?

   a. Chance

   b. Chanticleer

   c. Presley

   d. Trumpeter

97. In *Thumbelina*, is Jaquimo a fish or a bird?

98. What is the name of the prince in *Thumbelina*?

99. What does Gnorga order done to the troll she catches making flowers grow in *A Troll in Central Park*?

   a. Banished to Australia

   b. Put in prison

   c. Turned to stone

   d. Set adrift in a lifeboat

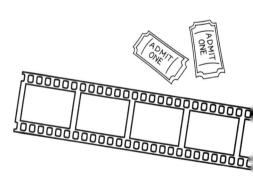

100. Who are the two children in *A Troll in Central Park*?

    a. Gus and Rosie

    b. Billy and Teddy

    c. Sidney and Nancy

    d. Eddy and Flo

101. Which of the following is not a main character in *The Pebble and the Penguin*?

    a. Hubie

    b. Marina

    c. Rocko

    d. Daisy

102. What is Rodney's metallic last name in *Robots*?

103. What are the misfit robots called in *Robots*?

    a. Outsiders

    b. Rusties

    c. Clankies

    d. Boltless

104. In *Ice Age*, is Sid a wooly mammoth or a sloth?

105. In *Ice Age*, what kind of animal is Diego?

106. What color hat does the lead human in *Curious George* wear?

107. In *Cats Don't Dance*, is Danny trying to be a star on Broadway or in Hollywood?

108. Which of the following is not a song in *The Swan Princess*?

a. "This Is My Idea"

b. "Far Longer than Forever"

c. Princesses on Parade"

d. "Truth is Never Easy"

109. What is the name of the prince in *The Swan Princess*?

110. In *Charlotte's Web*, what kind of animal is Wilbur?

111. In *Charlotte's Web*, what kind of animal is Templeton?

112. What kind of animal is the title character in *Balto*?

113. Which of the following is not a suspect in *Hoodwinked!*?

a. The Wolf
b. The Woodsman
c. Chief Grizzly
d. Granny

114. What kingdom does Milo visit in *The Phantom Tollbooth*?

    a. The Kingdom of Truth

    b. The Kingdom of Wisdom

    c. The Kingdom of Left Behind

    d. The Kingdom of Krichton

115. In the *Wallace and Gromit* animated films, which one is the dog: Wallace or Gromit?

116. What is the Viking boy's name in *How to Train Your Dragon*?

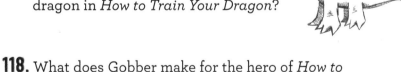

117. What is the nickname for the trained dragon in *How to Train Your Dragon*?

118. What does Gobber make for the hero of *How to Train Your Dragon*?

EXTRA CREDIT!

1. Who was the exclusive seller of Atari's *Pong* game?

    a. Wal-Mart

    b. K-Mart

    c. Sears

    d. Macy's

2. What year did *Space Invaders* first invade arcades?

    a. 1976

    b. 1978

    c. 1980

    d. 1982

3. Which came first, *Asteroids* or *Pac-man*?

ANSWER KEY 1. c 2. b 3. Asteroids

4. The Nintendo Entertainment System was first known as:

   a. Famicom

   b. Gencon

   c. Playcom

   d. Gamicon

5. What is the name of the addictive game developed by Russian programmer Alex Pajitnov in 1985?

6. What year was the Nintendo Game Boy first released?

   a. 1986

   b. 1989

   c. 1991

   d. 1993

7. The highest possible score in *Pac-man* is:

   a. 1,010,101

   b. 1,111,120

   c. 2,222,240

   d. 3,333,360

8. Which came first, *The Sims* or *Tamagotchi*?

9. Which came first, Sony PSP or Nintendo's Wii?

10. Which came first, *Super Mario World* or *Super Mario Bros. 3*?

11. For what computer was the first John Madden Football game designed?

12. Which artist does not have a hit song featured on the first *Rock Band*?

a. Red Hot Chili Peppers

b. Kiss

c. Madonna

d. The Police

13. Which came first, *Myst* or *Halo*?

14. Match the villain to the video game:

1. GlaDOS		a. *Metroid*	
2. Mother Brain		b. *Mega Man*	
3. Bowser		c. *Portal*	
4. Andrew Ryan		d. *Resident Evil*	
5. Ganon		e. *Zork*	
6. Dr. Robotnik		f. *Sonic the Hedgehog*	
7. Dr. Wily		g. *Batman*	
8. Albert Wesker		h. *Zelda*	
9. M. Bison		i. *Ratchet and Clank*	
10. Joker		j. *BioShock*	
11. Covenant		k. *Mario*	
12. Lich King		l. *God of War*	
13. Grue		m. *Halo*	
14. Zeus		n. *Street Fighter*	
15. Captain Qwark		o. *World of Warcraft*	

15. Was Abraham Lincoln one of the original world leaders in *Civilization IV*?

16. In *Sims*, which gets you more money: being a Getaway Driver or a Con Artist?

17. In Sims, which gets you more money: being a Bank Robber or a Counterfeiter?

18. In *Sims*, which gets you more money: being a Smuggler or a Cat Burgler?

19. Which of the following is not a *Sims* career track in the base game?

a. Business

b. Entertainment

c. Adventurer

d. Medical

20. Where do the *Sims* live?

21. What language do *Sims* speak?

22. Which expansion came first: *The Sims: House Party* or *The Sims: Vacation*?

23. Which expansion came first: *The Sims: Superstar* or *The Sims: Hot Date*?

24. What game sold more copies for *Atari: Missile Command* or *Pac-Man*?

25. Which sold more copies for Wii: *Wii Fit* or *Mario Party 8*?

26. Which sold more for Wii: *Wii Party* or *Wii Play*?

27. Which sold more for Wii: *Wii Sports* or *Super Mario Galaxy*?

ANSWER KEY 21. Simlish 22. Sims House Party 23. The Sims: Hot Date 24. Pac-Man 25. Wii Fit 26. Wii Play 27. Wii Sports

227

28. Which sold more for PlayStation: *Tomb Raider II* or *Tomb Raider*?

29. Which sold more for PlayStation 2: *Final Fantasy X* or *Grand Theft Auto III*?

30. What was the code name for the Wii while it was in development?

a. Reaction

b. Revolution

c. Recreator

d. Recreationator

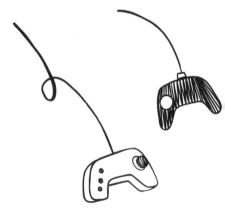

31. Complete the title of these Wii games:

1. *Active Life: Extreme _____*
2. *Alien _____ Bowling League*
3. *AMF Bowling World _____*
4. *Are You Smarter Than a 5th Grader: Make the _____*
5. *Backyard Sports: Sandlot _____*
6. *Batman: The Brave and the _____*
7. *Big Brain _____: Wii Degree*
8. *Bratz: Girlz Really _____!*
9. *Cabela's Big Game _____*
10. *Call of Duty: Black _____*
11. *Celebrity Sports _____*
12. *Doctor Fizzwhizzle's Animal _____*
13. *Donkey Kong Jungle _____*
14. *Kidz Bop Dance _____*
15. *Kirby's Return to _____*
16. *Legend of Zelda; Skyward _____*
17. *Mario and Sonic at the _____ Games*
18. *MySims: Sky _____*
19. *Pet Pals: Animal _____*
20. *Pirates vs. _____: Dodgeball*

32. Which of the following is not a Super Mario game for Wii?

   a. *Super Mario Galaxy 2*

   b. *Super Mario All-Stars*

   c. *Super Paper Mario*

   d. *Super Mario Indestructible*

33. Which of the following is not a Tony Hawk game for Wii?

   a. *Tony Hawk's Downhill Jam*

   b. *Tony Hawk: Shred*

   c. *Tony Hawk: Ride It Alone*

   d. *Tony Hawk's Proving Ground*

34. Which Wii game was released first in the *U.S.*, *Super Swing Golf* or *Madden NFL 07*?

35. Which Wii game was released first in the *U.S.*, *Brunswick Pro Bowling* or *MySims*?

36. Which came first for Wii, *Lego Indiana Jones: The Original Adventures* or *Lego Star Wars: The Complete Saga*?

37. Which came first for Wii: *Lego Batman* or *Lego Harry Potter*?

38. The designer of *Angry Birds* is from:

  a. England

  b. Finland

  c. Congo

  d. Ecuador

39. What color are the birds at the initial levels of *Angry Birds*?

TURN THE PAGE FOR A TRUE-OR-FALSE LIGHTNING ROUND!

HERE'S HOW TO GRADE A GROWN-UP:

0-5 QUESTIONS RIGHT: *Go Back to Second Grade!*

6-10 QUESTIONS RIGHT: *Nice Try... But Time to Repeat Grade Three!*

11-20 QUESTIONS RIGHT: *Lucky for you, Fourth Grade Wasn't So Bad— Back You Go!*

21+ QUESTIONS RIGHT: *Congratulations! You Might Be Ready for Middle School!*

AFTER-SCHOOL ACTIVITIES: LIGHTNING ROUND!

1. True or false: Super Mario Bros. is a spin-off from the game *Donkey Kong*.

2. True or false: J.K. Rowling's given names are Joanne Kathleen.

3. True or false: Katy Perry's real name is Katheryn Elizabeth Hudson.

4. True or false: Snoopy has a sister named Snippy.

5. True or false: Snoopy has a brother named Marbles.

6. True or false: In Disney's *Cinderella*, the stepsisters are named Drizella and Ariella.

ANSWER KEY 1. True 2. False—she has no middle name. 3. True 4. False 5. True 6. False—Drizella and Anastasia

7. True or false: The villain in *A Bug's Life* is General Mandible.

8. True or false: In *Toy Story 2*, Buzz Lightyear is kidnapped by the Evil Emperor Zurg.

9. True or false: The ladybug in *A Bug's Life* is male.

10. True or false: *Beauty and the Beast* begins with the words "Once upon a time."

11. True or false: In Disney's *Cinderella*, the prince is never named.

12. True or false: The Siamese cats in *Lady and the Tramp* are named Si and Am.

13. True or false: Dumbo's mom's name is never mentioned.

14. True or false: Drizella, Flora, and Tremaine are the fairies that raise Princess Aurora.

15. True or false: In *The Princess and the Frog*, Mama Odie can't speak.

16. Bugs Bunny said, "What's up, Doc?"

17. True or false: A dog returns from the dead in *All Dogs Go to Heaven*.

18. In "The Chipmunk Song," the present that Alvin really, really wants is a basketball

19. The song "Roar" by Katy Perry encourages you to embrace your inner cat.

20. The hit song "Happy" by Pharrell Williams was featured in the movie *Despicable Me*.

21. There are 24 keys on a clarinet.

22. Most guitars have 8 strings

23. A tom drum is larger than a bass drum.

24. The birds in the initial levels of *Angry Birds* are red.

25. There are 20 levels in each chapter of the initial release of *Angry Birds*.

IF YOUR GROWN-UP FAILED MISERABLY, HERE IS A READING LIST FOR BOTH OF YOU!

The Super Smart Science Series by April Chloe Terrazas

The Everything Kids' Science Experiments Book by Tom Robinson

The Cricket in Times Square by George Selden

Sarah, Plain and Tall by Patricia MacLachlan

The Penguin Group *"Who Was"* Series

Independent Dames by Laurie Anderson

Movie Night Trivia by Robb Pearlman

Family Fun Night by Cynthia Copeland

NEED MORE IDEAS FOR GETTING YOUR GROWN-UP UP TO SPEED IN SCHOOL? CHECK OUT THESE FAMILY-FRIENDLY WEBSITES, TOO!

HowStuffWorks.com

ScienceKids.co.nz

ReadingRainbow.com

GoodReads.com

Kids.NationalGeographic.com

BrainPOP.com

Scholastic.com/100books/

FamilyFunNight.org

About Applesauce Press

Good ideas ripen with time. From seed to harvest, Applesauce Press crafts books with beautiful designs, creative formats, and kid-friendly information on a variety of fascinating topics. Like our parent company, Cider Mill Press Book Publishers, our press bears fruit twice a year, publishing a new crop of titles each spring and fall.

Write to us at:
12 Spring St.
PO Box 454
Kennebunkport, ME 04046

Or visit us on the web at:
www.cidermillpress.com